THE
LONDON
LOOP

RECREATIONAL PATH GUIDE

THE
LONDON
LOOP

DAVID SHARP

Aurum Press

Ordnance Survey

Many people have worked towards creating the LOOP. On behalf of all those who will enjoy it in future years, our thanks go to Simon Walsh and Roger Warhurst for devising the idea, and to Alec Baxter-Brown, John Stern, Alister Hayes, Paul Mitchell, Helen Cocker, Bob Dunn, Linda Jedda, David Dench, Catherine Cairns and other stalwarts of the London Walking Forum, whose efforts turned it into reality.

First published 2001 by Aurum Press Limited
25 Bedford Avenue, London WC1B 3AT

A catalogue record for this book is available from the British Library.

ISBN 1 85410 759 3

3 5 7 9 10 8 6 4 2
2003 2005 2004 2002

Book design by Robert Updegraff
Printed and bound in Italy by Printer Trento Srl

Cover photograph: *Enfield Lock*
Title-page photograph: *Five Arch Bridge, River Cray*

CONTENTS

Preface

For those visitors who know London only as Oxford Street, Big Ben and the North Circular, this book may surprise you, as it gives an insight into the real London that locals already know well and enjoy. London is a green city and the 150-mile walk described in detail in this guide will lead you through ancient woodland and historic parkland to canals, estuaries and picturesque villages.

The guide starts at Erith riverside, but this 'M25 for walkers' has the advantage that it can be started (and finished for that matter) at any point along the way. Only one of the 15 walks falls outside Travelcard Zone 6 and the entire route is conveniently peppered with tube stations and bus stops.

The guide has been written by one of the route's founding fathers, David Sharp. David has also written the official guide to that other popular London greenway, the Thames Path National Trail. David is a Londoner and sits on the executive of the London Walking Forum, the official body that has co-ordinated the London Boroughs in order to develop and promote many initiatives for the benefit of pedestrians over the last ten years.

The Boroughs have reassuringly signed the route for the most part with a distinctive kestrel waymark and have worked hard to remove obstacles and improve the experience along the way. I recommend it to you, particularly if you wouldn't normally consider yourself a walker – London, as I discovered early on in my life, is best enjoyed on foot.

Ken Livingstone
Mayor of London

How to use this guide

This guide is in several parts.

First by way of introduction, a brief account of how the London LOOP came to be devised by the London Walking Forum, and the progress of the concept so far. Then, because the walk takes you exploring the outer edge of the capital, it gives some clues as to how London developed, including some stirring tales of the battles that saved many of the green spaces we enjoy on the walk. The LOOP has quite a story to tell.

Second, some guidance on walking the LOOP, and especially how to make best use of London's public transport to access it.

Then, a complete description of the walk itself, divided into 15 sections and illustrated with 1:25 000 scale maps, specially prepared by the Ordnance Survey® from their 1:25 000 Explorer™ maps. With text and maps on facing pages, you should find it easy to follow the LOOP, whether the section you are on has been signed and waymarked or not. Special features of interest have been numbered both in the text and on the maps. Letters have been used in the same way, to identify key points along the route. Cafés and toilets have been identified on or very near the route, and also public houses in locations where they will be most useful to LOOP walkers. Every section begins and ends at a public transport point, and any necessary links are described and shown on the maps.

Finally, the Useful Information section tells you more about Travelcards and the public transport links to the LOOP, organisations involved with walking in London, and further reading.

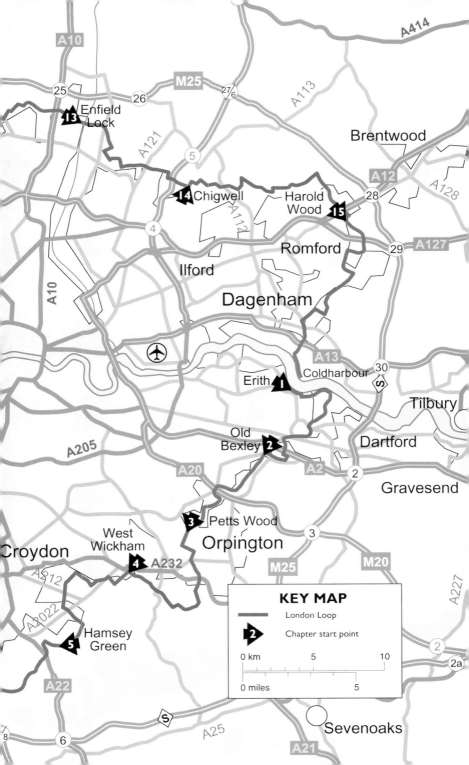

KEY MAP

London Loop

Chapter start point

0 km 5 10

0 miles 5

Introduction

Can London be anywhere near? The LOOP takes a peaceful woodland path along the edge of Oxhey Woods.

Discovering London's green edge

Many people can't believe the LOOP when they first meet it. Can all this glorious countryside truly be within the London boundary? The answer tells us much about how London has grown, and how so many green spaces have been saved for us, even while urban sprawl has threatened to engulf everything within reach. LOOP stands for London Outer Orbital Path – a prosaic enough title for such an inspiring concept, and it is truly the brainchild of the London Walking Forum, its brief history closely related to that of its proud parent.

Back in 1990, a mixed bag of enthusiasts found themselves sitting around the conference table in the Countryside Commission's newly opened London office in Kingsway. Some were local authority officers, others mere private individuals – but each had one passionate interest that brought them together: the creation of a green walking route somewhere within London. It was intended to be a one-off meeting, just an opportunity to pool experiences and talk over mutual problems. But by the end of day, everyone could sense the glimmer of a shared vision – something they might just possibly make happen by working together. Nothing less than the creation of a network of carefully prepared walks that could transform the lives of thousands of urban-dwelling Londoners by tempting them out to explore and enjoy the undiscovered green bits of their city. Thus the London Walking Forum was born.

It soon embraced all the London boroughs and every walking interest, and received a prestigious launch at the House of Lords in January 1993. As soon as the Forum got down to the mapping of all the potential walks, it was obvious that London offered unbelievable scope, with its surviving open spaces and secret ribbons of greenery tucked away behind the house tops, for the creation of walks, often deep in suburbia. But there was one further way to create a country-style route within everyone's easy reach. An ambitious way, circling around the very edge of London. It would involve 22 local authorities and several other bodies – a formidable task, now made possible as the Forum drew all these interests together for the first time.

So the LOOP began to evolve, first as a line on maps, then as a viable route on the ground as parties of ramblers were sent forth to evaluate and add their local expertise to the concept. Understandably, as it was their own creation, the Forum saw the LOOP as a model for all the best practice they would like to see on London walks. The LOOP, said the Forum, should be so easy and reassuring to follow, that even the complete beginner and his or her family could enjoy a few hours' walking with never a qualm about getting lost. As a walk within easy reach of all London's transport, the LOOP would encourage people to give their car a day off, too. In presentation, it should appeal to younger audiences and all those minority groups within the community with a message that the LOOP is for them, and they will actually enjoy this brief escape from inner-city drabness. The LOOP literature and interpretation boards are radical in reflecting this image, even to the extent of using deliberately 'unmaplike' graphics, to avoid putting off all those people who insist they cannot read maps! User surveys have already indicated a high level of approval for this approach, so while the LOOP has obvious attractions to London's vast walking public, it is also seeking to attract a wider audience – folk who have never before ventured off the pavements into green fields and leafy woods.

Making progress

Having firmed up the route, the next stage was to design the signs to be used along the LOOP. Even the choice of a waymark logo led to arguments. What would best symbolise London's green spaces? The fox and the squirrel were early candidates, but loudly rejected with cries of 'Rodents ... pests!' by long-suffering countryside management teams. Finally the kestrel got the vote – the hunter you often see, if not recognise, hovering over the green areas of the LOOP in search of its prey.

Two sets of signs were devised. For rural settings a simple waymark disc could combine with traditional oak fingerposts, which would have a plastic panel inserted to carry the LOOP graphics – a happy mix of old and new technology. For urban sections of the walk, bigger waymarks and aluminium fingers would usually be strapped onto existing street furniture, to avoid clutter. At significant spots along the LOOP, big 'main' signs would show off the sheer scale of the project by quoting distances to several destinations, one being as far as 30 miles away. No ordinary walk, this! Links to nearby railway stations would also have their own 'link' signs, so as not to be confused with the main route. Distinctive round-topped information boards were designed to be installed at key points, to tell you a little about the place reached, and whet the appetite with a glimpse of where the LOOP would go next.

Most of the cost of signing the LOOP has to come from local-authority budgets, and for this reason you will find that some sections are signed today, while others are not. This is a constantly changing situation, so this guide makes no allowance for signing, giving you a comprehensive route description that will get you along

At Hamsey Green a LOOP information board and a main sign showing distant destinations demonstrate the sheer scale of this walk.

St Dunstan's, standing almost alone in Cranford Park, is typical of many fascinating country churches visited on the LOOP.

the LOOP whether it is signed or not. In any case, signs go missing, or mysteriously turn to point the wrong way, so the guide provides a reliable cross-check. It is also possible that, when a new section of the LOOP is signed, minor changes may be made to its line. So, if you meet LOOP signs that are confidently pointing you off the route described in this guide, it would usually be best to follow them.

The miracle of London's country

The LOOP line was planned to take in the best countryside while trying to ensure that every key point where you would want to join it or leave it was accessible with a Travelcard or, for London's lucky pensioners, a Freedom Pass. But London is an odd shape. Across the north, the urban boundary is easy to define; indeed it is significant that the LOOP touches on several Underground termini – Uxbridge, Stanmore, High Barnet, Cockfosters – the edge of London in every sense. South of the Thames, the pattern is much less certain, and coming to the Thames Valley, the LOOP can only cross by the most pleasant line it can find – the true outer edge of London's development would be somewhere out beyond Staines.

But by thus following London's edge, actually walking out the pattern, you gain fascinating insights both into how London grew, and how just a handful of enlightened citizens kept the growth in check. The LOOP here has a wonderful story to tell.

From the confines of a medieval city, London really began to spread into its surrounding country in the late 18th century, when a combination of better roads out and the growing grime of the city itself made it fashionable for the upper classes to acquire villas in the country. Even as far out as Monken Hadley, the LOOP can show you the country homes of wealthy city merchants and financiers who could afford the move out. But the working man could not move. In the early 19th century he had to live literally within walking distance of his workbench, tramping in every morning over the Thames bridges, a solid mass of marching humanity on foot. London could only begin to expand seriously through the arrival of decent and cheap transport. The horse omnibus came first – by 1850 there were 1,300 of them – followed by the horse trams. But the true seismic shift in London's shape came with the arrival of the railway lines, creating a new species of human being – the commuter. At first the working man still couldn't afford to travel, but by the end of the century, cheap early-morning workers' fares were transforming this. For a twopenny ticket you could travel 10 miles to or from your home. By an inevitable process, as one class moved out of town, the middle classes moved out further still, and London began to sprawl, octopus-like, each tentacle representing the line of a railway. During the 19th century the population grew from 900,000 to an alarming six million, and early planners were beginning to wonder how far London would eventually spread.

Of course, the sprawl was commercially attractive both to developers and to railway companies, especially when the Underground lines, first promoted to relieve congested city streets, began to reach out speculatively into the country. Only the Metropolitan Line seems to have fully exploited the profitable idea of buying potential greenfield sites, then sending the development value rocketing up by building railway access. But even in the 1920s, the delights of 'Metroland' were still being promoted with images of rural bliss, just

As the LOOP climbs towards the Holwood estate, views open up to a sweeping

expanse of countryside – all within the London Borough of Bromley.

down the line. It was all a sham – your little semi in the country was very soon surrounded by hundreds of others, and 'country' became the dreaded suburbia. The Central Line was probably the last of these electrified tentacles to reach out, and the LOOP meets its ribbon of development as it crosses the Roding Valley. As London's tube system started out to serve the City and the West End, its lines were mainly north of the Thames. There was fierce opposition, too, from lines that had amalgamated and begun to electrify as the Southern Railway, so it was natural for the tube to expand north rather than south. This is why the LOOP meets no Underground lines south of the Thames.

By the 1920s, there was such concern over all this uncontrolled growth that the words 'green belt' entered our language to represent an idea of protecting a belt of rural land around London, and maybe provide more land for recreation in the process. Some land was actually purchased to safeguard it, but it was only when Abercrombie put his positive ideas forward in the 1940s that the 'green belt' concept became a planning principle – a countryside where farming would continue, but building development would be banned. When you walk through sweeps of unspoilt countryside like Enfield Chase or the High Elms estate in Bromley, and marvel that all this can be on London's LOOP, just remember that this is greenbelt-protected land.

Battles of past years

Back in the mid-19th century, long before any enlightened greenbelt principles emerged to control the situation, any large tract of low-value land around London's edge was beginning to look attractive to speculators. The ancient common lands were the most vulnerable – just a few commoners to see off – and the vast expanses of Banstead Commons have a tale to tell that is typical of many others. In 1873 Sir John Craddock bought them and immediately set about buying up the commoners' rights as well. He planned for houses on Banstead Downs, and began selling off the topsoil, gravel and turf from the heath. A local committee had to fight an incredible 13-year legal battle before an act of 1893 appointed eight conservators to protect the Commons for all time. Today we cross Banstead Downs on the LOOP, profoundly grateful that this wild common remains, with the tide of housing lapping at its edges.

Surplus private land looked equally promising as a source of profit. South of London, for example, the big Selsdon estate was

Waterfowl enjoy the lake in Hornchurch Country Park, with Albyns Farm on the skyline – a tranquil scene by the LOOP in Havering.

broken up into smallholdings for sale in the early 1920s, and only the efforts of a hurriedly formed committee managed to save part of it as a nature reserve. At the same time, over in Havering, another big and richly wooded estate was being parcelled up into narrow strips and sold off for £30 a plot. New owners camped out and even ran up bungalows on their tiny bits of country, until the Greater London Council stepped in, bought the plots back, and restored the landscape of what is now a country park. The LOOP goes through both these estates.

But of all the colourful battles fought around London's fringe, that to save Epping Forest must take pride of place. A perambulation of its bounds in 1640 declared this vast hunting forest to cover 60,000 acres. By 1851, only 6,000 acres remained open – the rest had been quietly enclosed by the lords of the manors all around, taking away the commoners' rights in the process. When yet another vast area was fenced in the Manor of Loughton, one old forester, Thomas Willingale, wouldn't stand for it. On St Martin's Day, 11 November, at midnight, as required by tradition, he set out with his two sons to pull down the fences on Staples Hill and strike an axe into the trees in exercise of common rights. For this, they were charged with malicious trespass and sentenced to two months' hard labour.

This outrage led to the whole issue being taken up, and when the newly formed Commons Society ran short of funds, the Corporation of London took over, having discovered that they owned a small patch of forest land for a cemetery, and were thus able to act for all the commoners. After years came a famous victory, when the Court of Chancery ruled that all the enclosures made since 1851 were illegal, and fences had to come down. In 1878 Parliament handed a full 6,000 acres of restored forest into the care of the Corporation, and four years later the streets of Chingford were transformed with loyal decorations as Queen Victoria came to hear her forest declared open and dedicated to the enjoyment of the people for all time. As you walk the LOOP through the glades of Hawk Wood and gaze over the panorama of treetops beyond Chingford Plain, remember the Willingales in their damp cells. One son developed pneumonia and died – a high price to pay for our freedom to walk.

The LOOP has further cause to be grateful to the Corporation of London. In that same year of 1878, Parliament also approved an Open Spaces Act, empowering the Corporation to take over land within 25 miles of the city for the purposes of public enjoyment. Under this Act, they now own and manage a list of well-known spaces, but most remarkably a string of parks and commons along the Kent and Surrey borders, all crossed by the LOOP. Riddlesdown, Kenley and Coulsdon Commons and Farthing Downs together give us the finest downland walking in London – yet in the 1870s the lord of the manor was busy enclosing them and stripping them of turf and gravel. An action was won in defence of commoners' rights, but the issue was only finally resolved when all four commons, a total of 347 acres, were bought by the Corporation of London for £7,000.

In Bromley the LOOP crosses two other fragments of common land, Spring Park and West Wickham Common, where the big boards with their coats of arms tell us that we are on Corporation of London land. In its way, the LOOP is a celebration and a gesture of appreciation for all those enlightened deeds that have given us this inheritance of green countryside around London.

Typical of many fine houses passed on the LOOP, Forty Hall by Inigo Jones dates back to the 1630s and is now owned by Enfield Borough.

Walking the LOOP

Although it is within London, this is a country walk, often along typical country paths. It offers just about every kind of walking – stony tracks around the estuary, paths by riversides and through ancient woods, along towpaths, over broad downland and lush meadows. London's countryside has amazing variety, but don't expect prepared paths all the way, and don't be surprised if you meet mud when season and location make this likely. But, being within London, you can usually count on civilised amenities being close at hand. Pubs, and even the happy prospect of a cup of tea, tend to turn up more obligingly on the LOOP than on more remote country walks. And when you decide you've had enough walking for one day, there will often be a bus stop reasonably near, or even a station.

This guide divides the LOOP into day walks of reasonable length, and then suggests one or two points where you could possibly divide the walks further into half-day outings. Usually these are not the only points where you could break off the walk, just the most obvious ones, and a bus map will soon suggest others. At the start of each section we indicate the length of the walk along the LOOP itself, and any extra distance you need to add on to allow for station links at start and finish. But the distances we quote to a suggested 'break-off' point can be taken as the full walking distance if you take that option. The LOOP will also meet up with, and even follow, other signed London walks around its circuit. These walks will probably have leaflets or guides of their own, and the London Walking Forum can provide more information (see Useful Addresses, p.165).

Welcome refreshments ahead! The LOOP drops down through Hilly Fields Park, Enfiel

Reaching the LOOP

Although it follows a vast circle, the London LOOP is, for practical purposes, a linear walk. The great majority of users will be travelling out from their London base, putting in a day's walking, then returning home from a point further around the circuit. To make this easy and economically attractive, the LOOP has been planned to be accessed via a series of transport points, with almost all of these lying within the outer Travelcard Zone boundary. Thus, one Travelcard will take you out and back, with complete freedom to swap between Underground, bus, Tramlink or national railway, as suits you. London pensioners will know that their Freedom Pass gives them the same facility. You can read more about Travelcards and their Zones under Useful Information at the back of this guide.

th the old Rose & Crown pub in view.

THE
LONDON
LOOP

1 ERITH RIVERSIDE TO OLD BEXLEY

8½ miles (13.5 km) plus ¼ mile (0.4 km) of station link. You can leave the route at Slade Green station after 4 miles (6.5 km) or at Crayford station after 6 miles (9.5 km).

Every walk, even a grand circuit around London's edge, needs a satisfying start and finish point, and there can be no feature that meets the brief as emphatically as the broad Thames estuary. So you first set foot on the London LOOP at Erith station **A**. From the handsome little station house by the platform down from London, go right along the tiled approach road, bending left with it to go under a busy new main road. At an odd cobbled roundabout, turn right into Stonewood Road. This soon comes to another main road, which you cross, via the pedestrian crossing opposite the Swimming Centre on your right, to enter the Riverside Gardens.

So where, you begin to wonder, is the river? Turn right along the garden paths and soon, if you bear up to an obvious viewing platform, all is revealed. You are gazing over a glorious open sweep of the Thames, beneath vast skies and with just a scattering of small boats to give scale to the scene. Across the river the gentle downs that rise so temptingly are, in truth, rubbish – the grassed-over slopes of the Rainham landfill site. Barely visible beneath them is Coldharbour Point, where your walk

At Erith the public pier gives breezy views over the estuary.

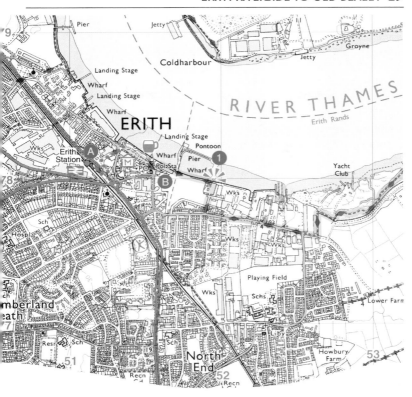

around the LOOP will eventually end. There can be few walks of this scale where you can see the finish point from the beginning!

In mid-Victorian times Erith tried valiantly to become a resort, creating gardens and a pier to bring the new-fangled pleasure steamers down from London. Burgeoning industry seems to have driven the pleasure-seekers away, but Erith is beginning to rediscover the joys of being beside the Thames, as you will very soon see. Follow the paths until the gardens end, then continue up the High Street to the Cross Keys pub. Immediately beyond the pub turn left to walk beside the car park **B** and down flights of steps to a new riverside promenade. Here the Deep Water Wharf has 'gone public' as a breezy pier **1**, taking Erith folk out over the mud to the low tide line. Seagulls swoop, gay flags add a cheerful flutter – only the bandstand is missing!

Where the promenade ends turn up right, go through the bollards and up to a main road, Manor Road. Turn left around the Royal Alfred pub and follow Manor Road, watching out for lorries and forklift trucks emerging from the industrial sites. A typical, dusty Thames estuary environment this – unchanging, except that the scrap-iron business now gains some environmental respectability as 'metals recycling'. The industry ends abruptly, and ahead you are gazing over the Crayford Marshes, rough grazing criss-crossed by dykes and occasional lines of scrub. In the distance rises the single chimney of Dartford Power Station, and beyond it, as though someone had drawn a thin arc of pencil line across the horizon, runs the Queen Elizabeth II bridge. Its span is so vast that you can barely detect the traffic crawling across it.

Turn left here on a metalled drive **C**, then right as it meets a fenced storage area. Keep ahead now, over a steel stile by a gate, and take to the raised causeway track across the marshes. Your aiming point is over to the left – the linked girder towers on Crayford Ness **2**, one carrying a beacon, the other a constantly rotating radar aerial. Here, briefly, you can capture the true estuary feel – the sense of sheer space and wildness. Shaggy piebald ponies still graze here, often tethered on your path, where the grass is greenest. A kestrel may well be hovering overhead, a symbolic welcome to the LOOP.

Beyond the Ness, your track soon comes to the mouth of the River Darent. Ahead is the creek flood barrier **3**, looking like an early mock-up of Tower Bridge in concrete. Cross its service road via two stiles and continue by the Darent, noting the lush reed beds and the waterfowl that hide there, rather than the stacks of scrapped cars to your right. But maybe these crumpled wrecks are another appropriate welcome to the LOOP. This walk is not very fond of cars!

Soon you come to a parting of ways **D**, *where a gravel track leads off rightwards towards Slade Green and its station.* Our way continues as a grassy track beside the Darent, until the waters divide and we find ourselves following the River Cray. With industry looming ahead again, go through another steel stile by a gate, turn right briefly, then left into a rough road **E**, where you may be dodging puddles and the occasional lorry. Dip under the railway, soon taking a left fork to come up to a busy road, the A206, beside the Jolly Farmers pub.

Cross the main road at pedestrian lights directly opposite the pub, then go left again over the Cray, and through a barrier onto a track beside the river **F**. Already the Cray has changed in character. Willows overhang the water, lush vegetation crowds in, including some spectacular giant hogweed in season. Coming up to a road, turn right and cross the river again, then left into Barnes Cray Road. Where this road turns right, keep ahead on a track **G**, with the Cray to your left. A sad stretch this – even the Cray has a melancholy feel as it flows unregarded by a run of backyards.

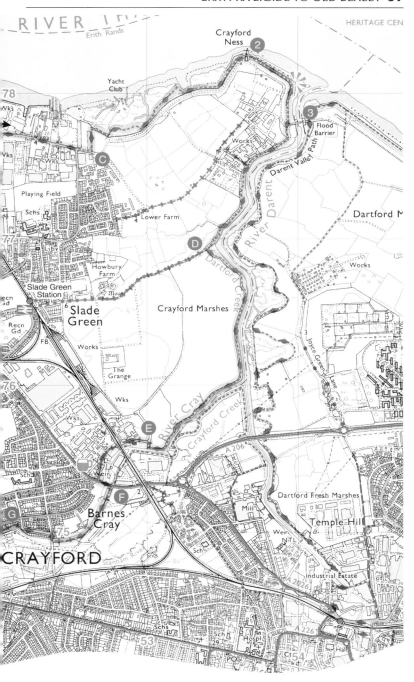

The red-brick 1640s half of Hall Place looks across its gardens to the placid River Cray in Bexley.

You think of streams that add beauty and a rural touch to urban lives, and you wonder why these houses turned their backs on little Cray.

Where the track ends, keep ahead on a footpath by the river, up to a road and shops at Crayford. An important spot, this, where the Roman Watling Street forded the Cray. Turn left to cross the Cray, then over the road to take a paved path in the tiny waterside garden (*there are toilets here*). When your path leaves the garden, turn right to cross the main road at pedestrian lights literally above the Cray **H**, and take the London Road with the big Bear & Ragged Staff pub over to your right. (*If, instead, you turn left after crossing and walk down Crayford Road past the town hall to turn right into Station Road, this will bring you to Crayford station.*)

Keep along London Road, crossing another busy road via pedestrian lights, then fork left into Bourne Road. As you come to a big garage, note the slender columns at the corners of their forecourt, decorated with shells and delicate fern motifs. Here stood the Crayford cinema, and these columns supported its canopy. Immediately beyond the garage, go left through a kissing gate **I** into open fields and walk down the left-hand boundary to find a grass path beside our old friend the Cray, at the bottom. Now a happier Cray flows through a parkland landscape. The path brings you to the hedge bounding Hall Place gardens, and while the LOOP turns left over the footbridge here, a diversion rightwards to skirt around the hedge brings you to Hall Place itself, with toilets, a café and the Jacobean Barn pub. Hall Place **4** is a delight – even though it would give any contemporary planning committee nightmares! Two building styles, 100 years apart, join together here in outrageous fashion.

This was the kind of country estate much prized by prosperous City merchants, and Sir John Champneis built the stone half as a hall house around 1540, using local monastery fragments for material. Three years earlier he had been Lord Mayor of London. Another wealthy City figure, Sir Robert Austen, bought the house in 1640 and doubled its size with his red-brick extension. Now council-owned, the gardens by the Cray make a fine setting for the house. The topiary, especially, is great fun. Like us humans, the heraldic figures have got fat in old age. The White Lion of Mortimer has become a chubby teddy bear, while the griffin seems to be wearing a rucksack rather than the eagle wings he started with.

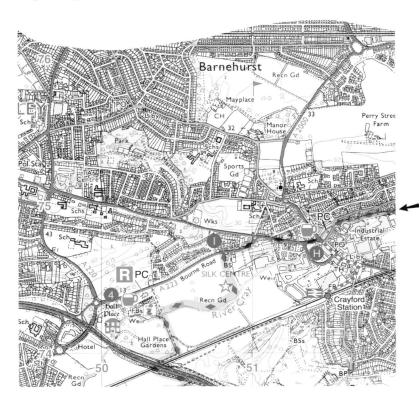

But enough of this frivolity. Skirt round the garden wall again, back to the footbridge over the Cray **J** and cross it, going left for a few paces, then right again to follow the hedge on. Cross a second footbridge over a lesser and usually dry channel of the Cray, then, when the hedge turns right, bear right across the grass to a kissing gate and steps up to a main road, the A2. Turn left beside the road to cross the railway line, then drop down the long, sloping path beyond. At its foot, turn acutely left on a path which goes under the road beside the railway, then turns left. Where the paths fork, keep right on the lower way, eventually to go right over a big stile **K** onto a path that follows the edge of Churchfield

St Mary's Church, Bexley, has 12th-century features, but the most distinctive feature of all is the odd octagonal cap on the spire.

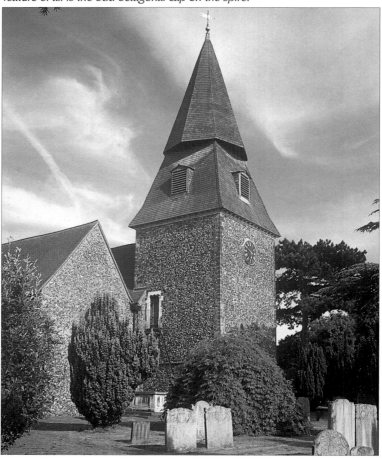

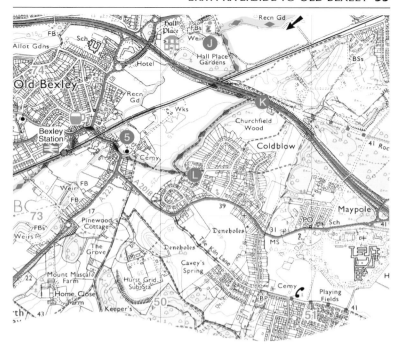

Wood, with its ivy-clad trees rising to your left and open fields to your right. Watch your head – some of those trees drop low across the path!

Through a kissing gate you come to a metalled crossing path **L**, where you turn right. It leads down beside the churchyard to St Mary's Church, Bexley **5**. Oddest feature here is the shingled spire which starts off as a pyramid, then has an octagonal bit perched on top. Maybe the planning committee that allowed Hall Place through was let loose on Bexley spire! Bear left, then right to take the main road. The first house you pass beyond the church is High Street House of 1761, a simple structure in yellow brick with a handsome portico. This was the home of John Thorpe, the Kentish historian. Pass opposite the big and rebuilt weatherboarded mill on the Cray, and under the railway bridge to a three-way road junction. You bear left here to keep along the High Street, but traffic is often so tricky that you may prefer to use the pedestrian crossing to your right before-hand. There are several pubs around this junction, and a drive on the left along the High Street soon takes you up to Bexley station.

Just before the station drive, at a corner by the Railway Tavern, the next LOOP section sets off to the left up Tanyard Lane.

2 OLD BEXLEY TO JUBILEE PARK

7¼ miles (11.5 km) plus ½ mile (0.8 km) of station link. You can leave the route at Foots Cray after 2½ miles (4 km) or at Queen Mary's Hospital after 3½ miles (5.5 km).

Setting off from Bexley station **A**, you are only two minutes away from the LOOP route. From the exit by the station house, drop down the approach road, turn right in the main road and, in just a few paces, go right into Tanyard Lane just before the Railway Tavern. *Already, you are on the LOOP.*

The lane bends and goes under the railway, now as a modest track. It follows the railway for a while, then bends left to join a rough lane leading to Bexley Cricket Club. Walk on in front of an isolated terrace of tile-hung houses, then ahead on a track that climbs over a landfill area. They are still dumping on this site, a one-time gravel working, but once your track is past the piled rubble it comes out onto a high plateau with views ahead and a kind of wild attraction. The clear way eventually drops steeply past an old, battered relic of a kissing gate, and runs between fields towards the houses beyond. It passes a red-brick pumping station to enter a road then, just

The Cray forms an ornamental lake spanned by Five Arch Bridge.

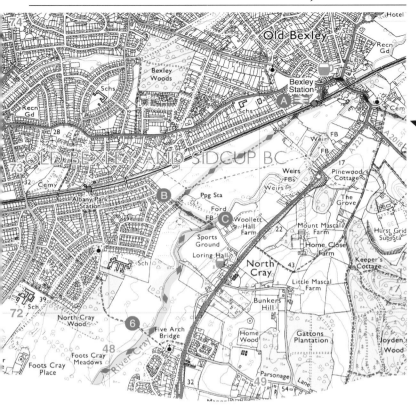

beyond the first semi-detached house on the left, you turn left onto a walled path **B**. Soon it runs between fences down to a footbridge over the River Cray.

Cross and turn right to follow beside the stream **C**. A perfect stretch of river scene follows, with the clear water of the Cray burbling along over its gravel beds. The tranquillity is marred only slightly by the distant rumble of traffic and an occasional screech from the parakeets that have colonised the tall trees hereabouts. The visual climax comes as you reach Five Arch Bridge **6**, where a weir beneath its arches has spread the waters of the Cray into a lake, beloved of mute swans, dabchicks and other waterfowl. Lake and bridge, built around 1780, clearly served as a landscape feature in the grounds of the now-departed Foots Cray Place.

Keep on through Foots Cray Meadows, with the Cray still to your right. The path swings away from the stream briefly to cross a culverted tributary, then returns to the bank. Eventually you go through a kissing gate and across the Cray via a little brick arch **D**. Keep ahead for 70 paces or so, then bear left on a path that takes you to the left of the church of All Saints **7**. Keep on along an open grass area to its end, then bear up rightwards to join the road, Rectory Lane. Go left in the road, along to the Foots Cray crossroads.

Cross here, to keep ahead along Cray Road. *(Just to your right is a bus stop, with services to Sidcup, Eltham, Lewisham, etc).* Take the second turning on the right, Suffolk Road, and at its very end go left on a path beside a tall hedge with playing fields to your left **E**. Where the hedge ends, turn right through concrete bollards onto a broader path across rough grazing fields. You pass the modest little football pitch where Cray Wanderers play, then bear left as you come to houses. The path bends several ways, then reaches open fields as the houses end. Go right up the bank **F** now to climb a grassy slope with a last, broad view over the Cray Valley opening up behind you. As you climb, aim for the giant redwood trees that stand majestically at the top of the hill, passing left of a play area to reach the handsome red brick of Sidcup Place **8**. The house is a mix of periods, with Victorian additions tacked around an 18th-century core – but perhaps its greatest attraction today is that, from council offices, it has now been happily converted into an inn.

Walk along the short garden terrace then, where it ends, turn right over the grass to follow a little tiled path beside their walled garden. Passing tennis courts you are on grass again, turning left at the main road to walk either on the pavement or more pleasantly on the open grass alongside. Pass the busy hospital entrance, then the bus stops alongside. *(Buses run from here to Sidcup station or Bromley, Bexley, Erith etc – lots of people come to Queen Mary's Hospital.)*

Ahead, we have to negotiate a complex two-level junction where the A20 meets the A222, but, fear not, our need has been provided for. Beyond the bus stops, a cycle and pedestrian route drops down to turn right and duck under the first road, then loops up, with steps for a short cut, to cross over the central road traffic. Then it dives down again for a repeat performance before our route goes under a final carriageway and you turn left up to road level again, bewildered but unharmed. On surfacing, keep ahead beside the road for a few paces, then right over a stile **G** with a deep sense of relief, into the greenery of Scadbury Park.

Take the path ahead, which soon bears left as a track through a belt of trees. It drops and joins another track to continue, still largely in trees. When a second track joins, keep ahead on a roughly surfaced way, then through a kissing gate into the open with a most satisfying vista over the fields of Scadbury Park to your right. Bear right at a little pond with platforms where local children come to dip into the crawly pond life, then, where the track ends, turn sharp left to follow the 'Scadbury Park Circular Walk' sign. Soon after meeting a chainlink fence on your left, turn right onto a path **H** that leads through the fine woodland of the park. At the top of a steep little rise, a path on the right will take you on a brief detour to visit the moated site of the manor house **9**.

Here, in the 13th century, the de Scathebury family built their first house and gave their name to the park and manor. The Walsinghams lived and entertained here through Tudor times. Their house was pulled down in the 1730s, and today this must be one of the most bewildering of archaeological sites anywhere. The reedy moat and some of its boundary brickwork are genuinely ancient, but what do we make of all those runs of suspiciously modern brick, or that chimney breast? It seems that, in the 1930s, they laid bricks to mark out the old foundations, and even had a stab at recreating the medieval hall with ancient timbers – the chimney was part of this venture.

Having taken you along the moatside, the path returns you to the main track to continue along the LOOP. After an enjoyable woodland

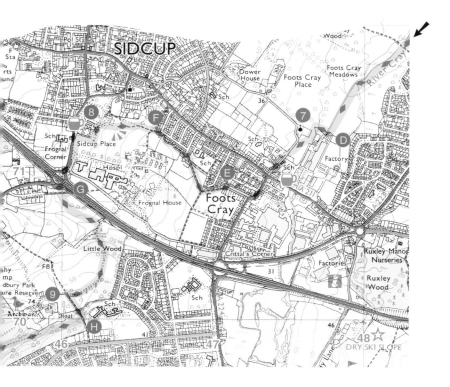

The LOOP takes a sylvan path through the woodland of Scadbury Park, with the further delights of Petts Wood up ahead.

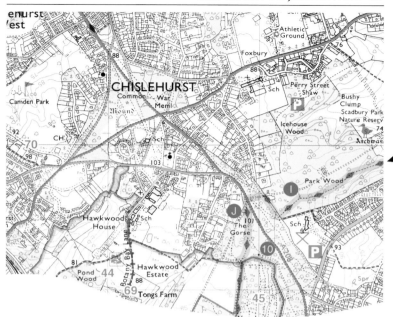

walk you pass a vast old oak with steps on the path beneath its lopped branches. Now you are in a birch wood, coming to a triangular meeting of paths with a bench to your left. Keep ahead still for a few paces, but then bear left off the track on a path **I** that soon goes through a wooden barrier to join another main track. Bear right here, then soon left on a metalled crossing drive to a main road, the A208.

Cross carefully to take the track opposite, beyond a barrier. Very soon you fork left on a woodland path **J** and keep resolutely along it. But there's something intriguing up ahead. Look out for an open triangle of grass with paths branching off, and a 'National Trust Petts Wood' sign on the path beyond. That's the way the LOOP goes, but retrace your steps a bit to take a path turning off to the left of your line of travel, just before you came to the grass area. It passes a tree stump on the left, crudely shaped into a kind of back-to-back seat. At this point go right, and you will find yourself in a woodland clearing with what looks like another tree stump at its centre. Close up, you realise that it is a granite column **10** to the memory of William Willett of Chislehurst, staunch campaigner behind the Summer Time Act of 1925. Circle round it, and you discover that it is, appropriately, a sundial, no doubt permanently and defiantly set on Summer Time.

Hidden away in a grove of Petts Wood you may find this granite sundial memorial to William Willett, campaigner for Daylight Saving.

Return to the grassy triangle and take the track ahead past the National Trust sign, soon walking with open fields to your right. Petts Wood, now an 88-acre (36-hectare) Trust property, is one of the many treasures around the LOOP saved for us by far-sighted citizens. Its name seems to derive from the Pett family, master shipwrights from Deptford who leased it in the 16th century, and doubtless made good use of its prime oak. Now it is delightful with a wider mix of birch, Scots pine and sweet chestnut, all thriving on its acid gravels.

After World War I an appeal raised the money to buy Petts Wood and thus save it from development.

Keep ahead on the main track as it drops gently downhill. At a junction of ways, you can just spot among the trees over to your right a second memorial stone **11**, this time remembering Francis Joseph Frederick Edlmann who saved this part of the wood for us in 1927. The track eventually arrives at an underpass under a railway line, but a little way before reaching it, turn right on a footpath **K** that twice forks left to keep near the line. It leaves the woods, then crosses the little Kyd Brook by footbridge, still following the railway. Soon you turn left to cross the lines by footbridge **L**, on a path that goes on over a single track line, over a road and then an impressive tangle of tracks – a trainspotter's paradise! Eventually it comes to a path junction at the edge of Jubilee Country Park. (*The next LOOP section continues ahead here, through the gate and onto one of the tempting paths in the park.*)

For Petts Wood station turn left on the pedestrian path **M**. It leads into Tent Peg Lane, from which you turn left in a road which bends round to the shops and pub of Petts Wood. The station turning is on the left, a short way down.

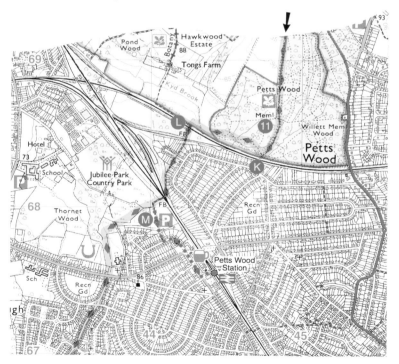

3 JUBILEE PARK TO WEST WICKHAM COMMON

9 miles (14 km) plus 1 mile (1.5 km) of station links. You can leave the route at Farnborough after 3½ miles (5.5 km).

This walk will surprise you with the sheer variety of countryside to be found within the Borough of Bromley. From Petts Wood station over-bridge **A**, set out by walking towards the shops and turning right on reaching them to follow Queensway. Where the main road traffic turns left, keep ahead on Crest View Drive, following it around a bend and then going right into little Tent Peg Lane. A short way down, take the path on the left into trees, keeping near the lane to reach a meet-ing of paths on the edge of Jubilee Country Park. *Here you join the LOOP route itself.*

Go left through the gate into the park to follow the metalled path for a few paces, then branching left on a less distinct path, over grass at first, to keep near the park boundary. We only skirt the edge of this attractive heath-like area, named to celebrate the Queen's Silver Jubilee in 1977. The path, taking on a gravel surface for a while, curves leftwards with playing fields away to your left and red-brick school buildings ahead. Reaching the school, you go through a gate **B** to bear right along their short drive to a road, Southborough Lane. Cross and take Oxhawth Crescent, opposite. Keep ahead, soon leav-ing the Crescent for Faringdon Avenue and on to its far end, where it meets a belt of woodland.

Turn left here, on a path into Crofton Wood **C**, a pleasantly wild tangle of oak and birch, managed by Bromley council. Ignore turn-ings to either side, and keep on the main path to cross a stream via a sleeper bridge. Soon after, at a meeting of paths, fork right and con-tinue to resist the temptation to turn off the main way, guided by a series of yellow-topped posts. You come eventually to an open glade **D**, where you fork right to pass a bench, then turn right again, back into the trees. Coming to a wider gravel track, turn right on it and pass a vehicle barrier to leave the woods. This track continues, with a stream to its left, to join a road at Crofton.

Although Crofton seems to have little claim to be a village, you will pass their village sign as soon as you turn left on the road. The Crofton Oak was indeed a nearby local landmark, but Emperor Hadrian might wonder how he came to be featured here! Pass the sign, cross the road, the A232, and retrace your steps a little to take

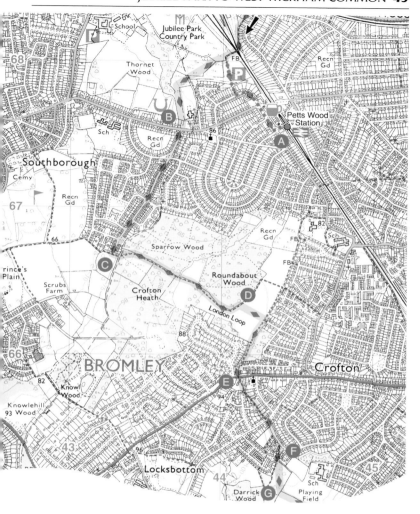

a path **E** almost opposite the sign, leading between garden fences. It crosses the top of a road and emerges at a road junction. Cross Lovibonds Avenue and take the road ahead, ignoring the first path signed to Farnborough, but taking the next path branching to the right, just before a little triangle of grass **F**. It goes through a barrier and on with houses to the right, then leaves them for a gentle climb up through Darrick Wood.

Emerging from trees at the top, go sharp left to take a track **G** with a line of posts and a grassy strip to its left, leading between playing fields.

This little path runs just above the ancient sunken way, Bogey Lane, giving you wider views over the rolling Bromley countryside.

It comes out, unexpectedly, on a hilltop with views south over the last of suburbia to the rising downs beyond. Bear right with the path at first, then leave it to drop down leftwards by a bench, taking the middle of three mown paths down the slope, towards trees and the sounds of traffic. If you've chosen right, you will come to steps and a fenced causeway leading out to a main road, the A21. Cross this via the island and take the footpath directly opposite, leading between houses and on along Gladstone Road into Farnborough village. *(Buses run from here into Orpington or Bromley.)*

Across the road, the George is clearly a big coaching inn, there since the 16th century. Farnborough seems to have been the first stop out of London along the coach road down to Tonbridge and Hastings. Along to your right, the New Inn has renamed itself the Change of Horses, to keep the historical associations alive. Its wooden horse trough has gone but opposite, appropriately, is a cottage labelled the Old Forge. Farnborough has one of the best village centres around the LOOP, but how much livelier the little High Street must have been when it echoed to the bustle and clip-clop of coaching trade.

At the triangular road junction, cross and take Church Road opposite. There are toilets a short way down, then a raised path leads through a lych gate into the churchyard of St Giles the Abbott **12**. The church stands high, which perhaps is why the present flint nave was rebuilt in the 1640s after storm damage. At that time they planted the yew by the west door – now vast, with a bench beneath it. Follow the metalled path right of the church and down through the churchyard. Coming into an open field, keep ahead down the left-hand edge, then into woodland. You may sense that the trees around you are becoming more exotic, and indeed you have entered the High Elms estate. Cross a lane and take the path opposite **H**, leading to a car park. Pass information boards, then bear left through a vehicle barrier on a track that joins the main drive of High Elms.

This grand 400-acre (162-hectare) estate, owned by Bromley Council since 1965, was the country home of the Lubbock family. Their classic Italian-style mansion was burnt down, and all that remains is the stable block and an almost indestructible feature – the Eton Fives Court **13**. This game was originally played against the walls of Eton College Chapel, with two pairs of players waxing aggressive with a hard ball. The rules required three playing surfaces and various hazards like buttresses and perhaps the occasional passing schoolmaster. The game was popular for a while, but this was one of the earliest courts, dating back to 1840. At that time, Sir John William Lubbock the Second enriched the grounds of his new house with specimen trees collected from around the world, and these you are seeing all about you.

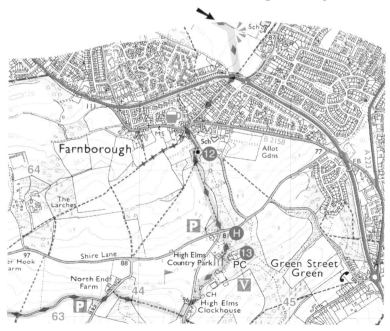

Just beyond the court, there are toilets in the stableyard. The drive you are following goes right, and ends at a car turning area. From here, keep ahead over the grass, through the garden terraces and down a grassy way between tall hedges to a kissing gate into another car park **I**. Keep ahead by the left-hand fence, to cross the golf-club car park and exit into a lane. Cross directly to the track opposite, but turn left immediately onto a path that follows the lane across an old orchard, now being replanted. Across the lane rises the white, weatherboarded tower of Clockhouse Farm **14**. As an early gesture towards Victorian efficiency, the bell was rung here to tell farm workers when their lunch break started and finished. Just beyond, you can see the white roof of an octagonal timber building, built around 1850 to house a donkey-wheel for pumping up water. One hopes that the donkey also had a lunch break!

Opposite the Clockhouse, turn right up a track **J** that climbs over the golf course, crosses a horse track via barriers, then drops to a lane. Turn left here, briefly, then right into an ancient hedged green way with the intriguing name of Bogey Lane **K**. Very soon you can go up steps on the left to take a path that runs just above the lane, with broader views and less mud. Eventually it drops down to the lane again. Keep to the hedged way, the middle of three paths ahead, as it bends and comes to a modest metalled road with another delightful name – Farthing Street. Turn right and follow it as it winds down to Shire Lane, far busier with traffic.

Here Wilberforce and the younger Pitt debated the abolition of the slave trade.

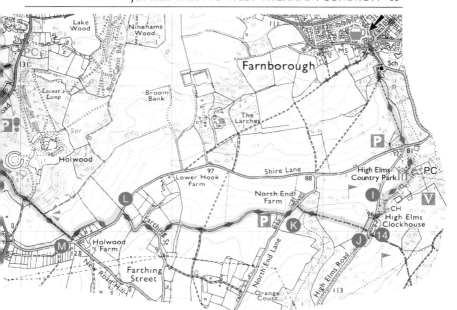

Cross and turn left on the path **L** just inside the field opposite, created as a permissive way to keep you off the road. Soon you cross a stile, then a second stile on the right, as the path continues beside a farm track.

On the hilltop plateau ahead, you are looking to the house of Holwood, a long white frontage with a Grecian portico, and doubtless a superb view down through the remains of Humphrey Repton's plantings, to the countryside we are walking through. At the top of the field go left over a stile, then right through a barrier onto a track **M** that climbs steeply towards the Holwood estate. Before entering the trees, look back for one last sweeping view over pastoral fields, and marvel that all this is in London.

The track brings you, breathlessly, to the summit clearing where stands all that remains of the Wilberforce Oak **15**. Here, William Wilberforce conversed with the younger William Pitt, Prime Minister and then owner of Holwood, to resolve on a parliamentary bill to abolish the slave trade. They met beneath an oak already ancient, and today only a shattered stump remains. A second old oak nearby points a couple of splintered spikes into the air – an appropriately Churchillian gesture to offer across the Vale of Keston. The commemorative stone bench set here in 1862 is firmly fenced off, but a simple wooden companion nearby looks far more comfortable, anyway.

The waters of the tree-ringed ponds on Keston Common form the source of the R

ensbourne, a spot even the Romans appreciated.

The path now drops gently to a road. Cross carefully to a path opposite onto Keston Common **N**, and very soon turn right on a track that drops down a dell to a car park. Cross this and take the steps on the far side, down to Caesar's Well **16**. The spring here, bubbling up from its brick-lined circle of pebbles, is the source of the Ravensbourne. As there is an Iron Age fort on the hill above it, this clear water was surely appreciated long before Caesar's time. Now the water flows into Keston Ponds, made in the early 19th century, it seems, to provide Holwood House with a water supply. Step over the water channel and walk beside the first pond, turning left to cross between the two ponds, then down steps to follow beside the second, now on your right. Coming to a road, cross and keep ahead with more ponds down to your right. (*There are toilets on the main road, to your right.*) Keep to the main track as it bends left in the woods, becomes metalled and leads into Lakes Road. Follow the road down to the B265 and the Fox pub at Keston.

Cross the main road at the mini-roundabout, then cross Fox Lane to take a roadside path on to a second roundabout. Continue into West Common Road, then immediately left on a track and, in a few paces, right on a path **O** that keeps quite near the road. Eventually you rejoin the roadside path, forking with it along Baston Manor Road. After a while it leaves the road to follow the common edge. You will pass your first Corporation of London board, proudly displaying their coat of arms in bas-relief, and proclaiming that you have reached West Wickham Common. It has been suggested that these boards have to be big to accommodate all the bye-laws on the back! Certainly, in 1892, they were strict – no cursing, swearing or improper language, no throwing of sticks or stones, and heaven help you if you were caught brushing a carpet!

The path comes near the road by houses, but cross over a minor road and keep on a footpath through a barrier and away from the traffic again. Follow the gravel track for a while, but when it swings away rightwards, keep ahead on a lesser path **P** that stays near the common escarpment. It drops down to join Gates Green Road, where stands another Corporation board and several of the incredible pollarded oaks, sometimes called the 'Domesday Oaks' **17**. One by our path still survives with four great trunks. A few paces on, a hollow stump stands surrounded by oak seedlings, its 'children'. Lopped year by year for their wood, these great trees could be 700 years old, or even more. An early walking-guide author, Walker Miles, paused here to point out the ancient oaks of West Wickham Common. Here they still stand, even more ancient now, by a hundred years.

The next LOOP section continues by turning left along Gates Green Road. For Hayes station, cross this road, then the main road via a pedestrian island ahead, to turn right over Coney Hill Road and walk back up the main road until a pathway goes sharply off on the left, with another odd name – Pole Cat Alley. This switchback path becomes Warren Wood Close, then joins a road. Take the second turning on the left, Station Hill, and at its bottom bear left for the shops, a big pub and the station.

4 WEST WICKHAM COMMON TO HAMSEY GREEN

8½ miles (13.5 km) plus ½ mile (0.8 km) of station link. You can leave the route at Upper Shirley after 4 miles (6.5 km), or Selsdon after 6 miles (9.5 km).

From Hayes station **A**, a short walk will bring you to the LOOP route. Leaving the station, turn right to cross Bourne Way via the pedestrian island, then left along the opposite pavement to start climbing Station Hill. Keep to Station Hill as it bears right, and you will soon find yourself on the edge of Hayes Common. Turn right here along Warren Road, and continue into Warren Wood Close, which sounds primly suburban but is here just an earthen way through the trees. It passes one or two houses and crosses the top of Holland Way, to become a narrower, metalled path – Pole Cat Alley. This odd switchback of a path swoops down, up and down again to arrive at a main road. Turn right, downhill, to cross Coney Hill Road, then left over the main road via an island and back up, to turn into Gates Green Road. *Here you join the LOOP, which drops down from West Wickham Common past the big Corporation of London board and the ancient pollarded oaks* **17** *across the road.*

A few paces further down Gates Green Road, turn right onto a footpath **B** between house gardens. Although so urban now, you will soon

The LOOP follows an ancient and well-trodden church path up to St John the Baptist, parish church of West Wickham.

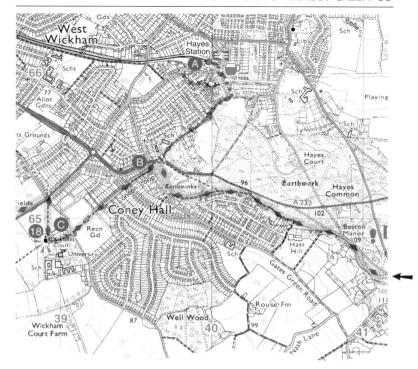

realise that this was one of a web of church paths leading to West Wickham parish church. As it comes to a crossing road, an old notice from a long-departed borough prohibits 'the riding of bicycles, tricycles or other similar machines'. Over the road, keep ahead up Church Drive, then through gates to follow a broad way between playing fields. A short way on, a little Dalek-like stone with a line over its top stands on the Greenwich Meridian, or 'the prime meridian of the world' as its faint inscription claims. Across another road, youthful voices often proclaim the near presence of St John Rigby College. Walk ahead towards the tower of St John the Baptist Church **18**, now visible through the trees.

The manor house, Wickham Court, can just be glimpsed with its tall chimneys over to your left, but college buildings cluster around it. Going through the lych gate, it is rewarding to walk ahead between the dark yews past the church just to enjoy the view from this hilltop churchyard, across the fields to the distant woods of Spring Park – our next objective. Otherwise, the LOOP turns right onto a path soon after going through the lych gate, dropping to a kissing gate **C** and then via a well-trodden fieldpath to another kissing gate by a busy roundabout. Turn your back on the traffic here for a moment, and look back to St John the Baptist silhouetted against the skyline. It would be difficult to put an age to most paths we use around the LOOP, but a church path like this would have been tramped out by Saxon feet, when the first church was built on the hill. One wonders how many have followed it over the centuries.

Cross Addington Road at the island to your left, go right into Corkscrew Hill but turn immediately left through a hedge gap **D** into Sparrows Den playing fields. This long sweep of grass has football pitches stretching into the far distance. Follow the left-hand boundary trees for a while, then bear right across the pitches towards the nearest corner of the woods. Spring Park Woods have been Corporation of London-owned since 1926, and the name seems to derive from the winter springs that rise and feed a pond by the woodland edge. At the corner you may spot a Corporation board in the trees, but do not enter the woods immediately – we aim for a higher path. Bear up rightwards on a path just outside the woods until, almost at houses, a stile on the left **E** leads into the trees. The path climbs still, then follows a right-hand fence along the highest ground. When the fence ends, keep ahead, ignoring crossing paths until another little wayside stone tells that you are leaving Bromley and entering Croydon. The stone was sited here in 1996 when this section of the LOOP was opened, and if you explore downhill a little you can still trace the old boundary bank that once separated Kent from Surrey.

Now you have crossed into Three Halfpenny Wood. Try explaining that to a younger generation! The track bears right, climbs again and

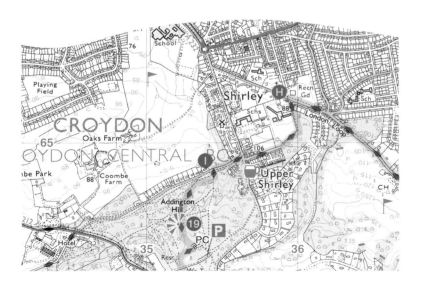

crosses a broader track to come out on the open grass of Shirley Heath **F**. Bear left along the edge of this grassy strip, through a thin tree belt and across the middle of a wider open space with houses in view to both sides. At the very far side, enter the trees again and almost immediately turn right on a broad, newly surfaced track. When the track comes near houses, leave it for a lesser path on the left **G**, soon forking left on a cross track which you soon realise is keeping just within the woodland edge. It meanders along with houses in sight to the right, eventually coming up to a main road, Shirley Road. Turn right along its nearside footway, almost a woodland path in places, especially where it passes little Foxes Wood. Hereabouts, it is best to cross to the other footway, continuing past the open grass of Shirley Church recreation ground. Opposite the children's play area, turn left on the path **H** into Pinewoods, another fragment of woodland. If you prefer the paths in the trees rather than the metalled way beside school playing fields, don't miss the point where the path turns right. It reaches the bottom of a road, which you follow up to the busy Upper Shirley Road, with the Sandrock pub on the corner.

Cross directly over, to take Oaks Road opposite. *(From the bus stop up the hill to your left, buses run into Croydon.)* Some way down Oaks Road, a gate on the left **I** leads into the woods. Turn right immediately on a path that keeps near the road for a while, then bears left on a climb that ends with an energetic scramble up uncomfortably gravelly steps to the viewing platform on Addington Hills **19**. The

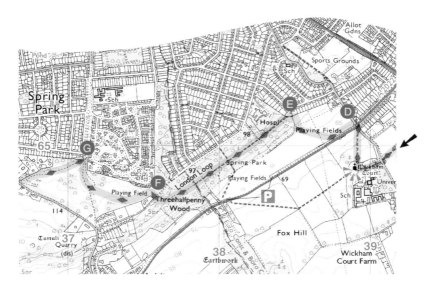

view is north, with a touch of civic pride, over central Croydon. The masts of Crystal Palace are very clear; there are suggestions that Windsor Castle and Epping Forest might be seen, and Croydon Town Hall is on the viewing list, of course. Having thus surveyed the London you have temporarily escaped from, turn and follow the main approach path to distant buildings, where you turn right **J**. *There is a restaurant here, with public toilets just to one side.*

Soon you fork left, then turn right on a crossing track. Just before the track comes to a steep descent, turn sharp left on a footpath that leads to Coombe Lane station on the Tramlink line *(with frequent services into Croydon)*. Cross the tracks, keeping a keen eye open for these swift, silent vehicles, then go left on a path that follows near the road, with new plantings to restore the scars of recent track work. Continue until you can cross the road via the lights at the Tramlink crossing, then retrace your steps to go through the gates into Heathfield Gardens.

A few paces in, fork left off the drive to take a log-lined path through the shrubbery, then down a flight of steps to a pond, charmingly situated in a dell. The house of Heathfield **20** is just visible to your left here and, especially in late spring when the azaleas are ablaze with

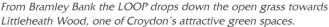

From Bramley Bank the LOOP drops down the open grass towards Littleheath Wood, one of Croydon's attractive green spaces.

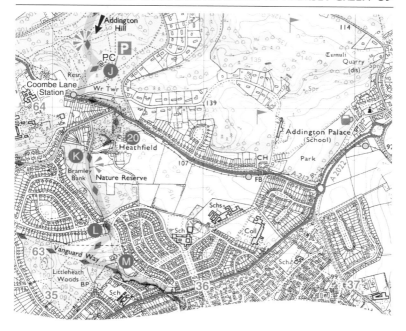

colour, the garden paths around may tempt you into exploring awhile. The LOOP climbs more steps to right of the pond, taking a right turn to enter a car park. Cross this, then in the lane beyond turn left downhill, and where the lane turns left, keep ahead into Bramley Bank **K**, a London Wildlife Trust nature reserve. Immediately, a tiny clearing gives a breathtaking view south-east across the fields to the distant high-rise blocks of New Addington, with an irresistible little log bench for sitting and admiring it all. Keep on by the left-hand edge of this ridge-top wood, leaving via a gate into an area of open grass. Bear right along the edge, through a gap in a barrier to take a metalled path to the left a few paces, then down the path **L** into Littleheath Wood.

Soon, a right turn brings you out onto another sweep of open grass. Walk down its centre, passing a log bench and going just above a group of five birches to enter the woods again on the left, by another log bench. A short way into the woods, turn left on an uphill track, then left along the hillcrest briefly before taking a path on the right **M**, dropping downhill again. It descends with houses to the right, then emerges at a grass strip with houses across the road. A way has been cleared just inside the trees down to a short path, beneath a pylon, leading out to Selsdon Park Road.

In evening light, the LOOP in pastoral mood takes a field-edge path from Farleigh towards Hamsey Green.

Turn left briefly to cross at the light-controlled crossing. *(A bus stop just beyond has services into Croydon.)* Walk back along the main road, and turn into Ashen Vale. Where this road bends right, an old bridleway **N** keeps ahead, its line carefully preserved through new housing as it crosses two roads and brings you to the gate into Selsdon Wood. This was part of the big Selsdon Estate – hunting and shooting country – until the early 1920s when it was broken up into smaller parcels, ready for the tide of suburbia to flood over it. A local committee managed to save these 200 acres (81 hectares) as a nature reserve and bird sanctuary, a stretch of ancient woodland we now walk through thankfully, which was given to the National Trust in 1936 with an agreement that Croydon Borough would manage it.

In the reserve go right for a few paces, then left on a broad path that climbs through the woods, ignoring crossing tracks, then drops to an exit gate with housing to the left and green fields ahead. You are right on the London boundary here, and indeed when you turn right to follow the old bridleway, Baker Boy Lane **O**, outside the gate, you are tracing the boundary. The little bluebell wood to your left, Puplet Wood, is in Tandridge, Surrey. Eventually the lane emerges from the woods and arrives at a main road by the entrance drive to Farleigh Court Golf Club. Keep ahead over the drive onto an often-muddy horse ride which follows the main road and finally joins it opposite Elm Farm **21**. A perfect farmstead this, simple brick with high-pitched roof and barns grouped around. No elms today, but plenty of mud as proof that it is still a working farm!

Cross the road and take the track to the left of the farmhouse. It runs between hedges, drops steeply to cross a broad, green valley, then climbs again and comes into open fields. Keep ahead, with an old field boundary and tree line to your left, to reach a rough stile **P** into a track, Kingswood Lane. Turn left here and follow the lane until, after passing a big country house, it becomes urban with the first houses of Hamsey Green. Coming up to a main road, the Good Companions pub stands on the opposite corner, *with the next LOOP section continuing down Tithe Pit Shaw Lane beside it.* But the shops of Hamsey Green are just to your right, and by the little green in front of the pub the bus stop has a frequent service into central Croydon.

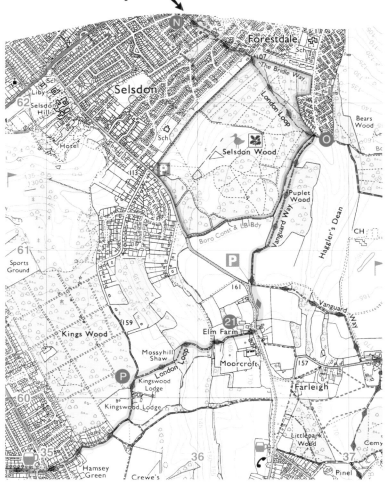

5 HAMSEY GREEN TO BANSTEAD DOWNS

10 miles (16 km) plus ¼ mile (0.4 km) of station link. You can leave the route at Coulsdon Common after 3½ miles (5.6 km), or at Coulsdon South station after 6 miles (9.5 km)

To join this section of the LOOP, you will probably be starting out from East Croydon station. It's a short walk round to the bus stop outside Fairfield Halls, from where the 403 service will take you to the stop just beyond Hamsey Green pond **A**. *Step off the bus and you are on the LOOP.*

Walk back to cross the main road at a pedestrian island, and go down Tithe Pit Shaw Lane, to the left of the Good Companions pub. Where this road turns left, continue forward past a gate, with a welcoming promise of open country before you. A board confirms it all – two local authorities and the Corporation of London have combined their properties to give us this grand sweep of open meadow and downland, from Riddlesdown, south to Whyteleafe.

Stride off into it, taking the track that crosses Dipsley Field ahead, then bends right to run beside a line of oaks, the vast Skylark Meadow dropping away leftwards towards the Whyteleafe valley. Along this stretch you pass a little concrete pillar **22**, a trig point used by the Ordnance Survey until recently for triangulation work. They usually turn up on high hilltops, and this is the only specimen we pass on the LOOP. Where the meadow ends **B**, turn left to follow a hedge, the valley instantly opening up before you. Through a kissing gate with hazel coppicing beyond, turn left to drop down the slope and via more kissing gates to join a stony track. This is the Old Riddlesdown Road, and in days when main roads went over the chalk downs rather than wriggling beneath them, this was a main coaching route to Lewes and Brighton. The fine ridge of Riddlesdown itself is up to your right, with grazing restored by the Corporation of London to keep its open grassland character. You may see their sheep in the enclosures here – the dappled brown-black of the Jacobs or the plainer Southdowns, chewing away. The old road drops in a steep-sided gully, over a railway bridge and down to join today's main road. An earlier version of the Rose and Crown pub, opposite, supplied fresh horses for the steep pull up towards London.

Cross the main road to take Old Barn Lane beside the pub, an unlikely turning that leads to a footbridge over the other railway line along this crowded valley. Cross it and continue over a crossing road, then steeply up New Barn Lane. Glancing back, you can see the chalk cliffs of an old quarry with a railway viaduct beneath it. Where the road ends, some serious climbing begins. First two short flights of steps **C**, then a longer run on the right leads up to Kenley Common. When you've got your breath back at the top, walk ahead by a right-hand hedge, over a crossing track and on into the coppiced woodland of the common. Where the broad track divides **D**, take the lesser track on the left, coming soon into an open grass area where your way is a mown path, diagonally leftwards across it. On the far side it cuts across a woodland corner and bears left, passing a big Corporation of London board, to leave the common via gates into a drive, Golf Road. But at this point it is worth diverting briefly to walk ahead to the common edge, over a horse ride and through a gate into some colourful recent history. You are on the edge of Kenley Airfield **23**, the last of London's Battle of Britain fighter stations to survive in its World War II form. To your left is the grass bank of a blast bay where Spitfires from one of Kenley's three squadrons sheltered. Way across the field, the officers' mess and one of the operations huts still stand. Today, Kenley is only a glider training school, and it is difficult to relate this peaceful scene with the crunch of Luftwaffe bombs and the roar of Merlin engines.

Swinging down from Coulsdon Common into Happy Valley, the LOOP treats you to some of the best chalk downland near London.

When Golf Road comes to a busier road, turn right, using the verge where possible, then go left on a footpath **E** just before the first house on the left. At a junction of paths go right and come almost immediately onto the open grass of Betts Mead with an unexpected line of children's swings to your left. Pass them by, and a little way on go left through a hedge gap into another field. Walk near the left-hand hedge, then, coming near houses and a lane, fork right to a hedge gap and steps down into the lane. *Just up the lane to your left is the Wattenden Arms pub.*

Cross straight over into an entry **F**, then immediately left over a stile. In the field beyond, the path curves right to join a left-hand line of fencing, and you aim for a white dome ahead – a small observatory **24**. To your left here are more overgrown bunkers and chunks of mysterious concrete, belonging to Kenley Airfield, just visible beyond them. Right beside the observatory you join a drive and follow it through a gate, forking right just beyond it on a narrow footpath **G** that drops to a meeting of ways. Here the route is ahead and downhill on an old track, Waterhouse Lane. When it comes to a road, cross and take Rydons Lane opposite, up to Coulsdon Common. Like many other commons we cross on the LOOP, Coulsdon has lost most of its character as rough grazing for a cover of oak woodland, but once two windmills stood just to your right on what must have been a suitably open, windswept height. Cross a road and a horseride to follow the broad track ahead through the trees, emerging soon at a main road. *A bus stop to your right across the road has services to Coulsdon South or East Croydon stations.*

Cross here and walk down Fox Lane, passing the Fox pub on your left, then a car park, to continue ahead on a track that gets rougher beside a vast open meadow with the strange devices of a 'trim trail' to your left. It drops and comes out on the slopes of Happy Valley, stones giving way to springy turf underfoot. Through a tree break you come to a viewpoint where you could picnic at a rustic table and drink in the panorama of chalk grassland, rising to Farthing Downs on the skyline – surely the finest view of its kind in London's country. Turn left to follow the vast, ancient hedgerow across the dry valley and up again to join a path **H** running just outside the line of woods. Further along it enters the trees and climbs the hillside to emerge on the wide ridgetop of Farthing Downs. *There are toilets here, by the car park across the road.*

To avoid putting signs into this sensitive landscape, the LOOP formally keeps to the road over Farthing Downs, but to enjoy them to the full, cross the road and take one of the tracks that follow the ridge over open grass – skylarks overhead and the view northwards opening over London. The climax comes when you reach the crossing point of old tracks, known as The Folly **25**. Here, in 1783, a local landowner crowned the summit with a grove of seven beech trees, of which only two remain, and one of them only a hollow stump, struck by lightning years ago. New young beeches

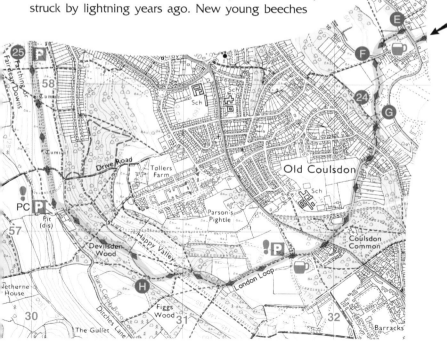

have been planted recently to restore the number. Stride on down the grassy track, and soon you will be passing big, circular mounds to your right – the remains of a major cemetery of 7th-century Saxon times. Only kings and great leaders were accorded barrow burials like this, but we will never know whose graves we are passing here. A little further down the slope a network of field banks was discovered in 1942 astride an ancient track – traces of the first Iron Age farmers to work this poor soil. From their time on, these downs have been grazed, and today the Corporation runs a herd of stolid deep-brown Sussex cattle to keep the grass short and the scrub in check. The 'spats' they wear are reflectors to make them visible to motorists.

Road and tracks finally leave the downs via a selection of gates, and you have an urban stretch to walk, across the Coulsdon Valley. You join a main road, then very soon turn left into Reddown Road and a little way down go right on a path **I** that leads down steps to a footbridge over the railway at Coulsdon South station. *There are trains from here to East Croydon and central London.*

Having crossed the lines, a path in front of the station house takes you down the bank to a light-controlled crossing of the A23 road. Cross and turn right to walk under the railway bridge, then fork left at the first traffic lights into Lion Green Road. At a second set of lights, several roads converge. Cross Chipstead Valley Road to take the second left-hand turning, Woodman Road. A short way up, just round a bend, take the path on the right **J** which bears left, crosses another set of railway lines and comes into Woodmansterne Road. Turn left and soon fork right as Woodmansterne Road begins a long, steady climb out of the valley. Where you enter Sutton it becomes Grove Lane; keep on along the grass verge and pass the Jack and Jill – a well-chosen name for a hilltop pub.

Soon after passing the pub, a separate track **K** branches away from the road, an old way sunk between high hedges. Look out on the left for an iron plate of 1898, marking the boundary of a now-departed district council. Shortly after, you pass through iron gates that once led into the Woodcote estate, and fork left, then left again after passing between steel posts. Across the fields to your right now, wherever you look, there are neat little semi-detached farm houses of a uniform black weatherboarding and white window frames – an intriguing sight. This is the Little Woodcote estate **26**, divided up into smallholdings in the 1920s by Surrey County Council in a worthy bid to give returning heroes from World War I a chance to become farmers. It never really worked, but some of the plots are still growing vegetables.

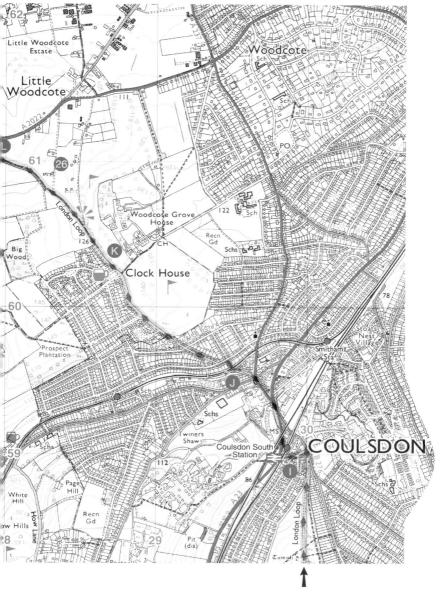

Walk on along a broad track, bearing right at a gate, with your eyes surely to the north where the LOOP gives one of its spectacular views over central London. Over a crossing track, look out for a stile on the left **L** into rough pasture land. A fairly clear path crosses to a stile in the furthest corner, where you turn left in Carshalton Road, watching out for its fast traffic. At the start of a bend, go right over a stile **M** to walk ahead beside the left-hand hedge until it turns away, then forking right to reach double stiles beneath the biggest trees across the meadow. Keep along the ridge of the next field, aiming for a lodge cottage, then over a stile and another busy road to take the drive ahead into Oaks Park **27**. *You will see a café and toilets over to your right here.*

The house of Oaks Park was demolished in 1960, but the Derby family, who took over the estate in the 1700s, gave it a colourful reputation as a hunting and racing centre, keeping staghounds and spreading the fame of Oaks Park far and wide with extravagant fêtes and parties. One race, The Oaks, took its name from the estate, and legend tells of the 12th Earl tossing a coin with Sir Charles Bunbury to decide the name for a new flat race. 'The Derby' won, and it is difficult to imagine those colourful crowds flocking to Epsom Downs to watch a race called 'The Bunbury'! The estate name was originally The Lambert Oaks. The Lamberts lived here from the 14th century and planted a grove of oaks, a few survivors of which can still be seen beside the main drive that goes left of the café. The park lost some 13,000 trees in the great 1987 storm, but wellwishers have planted many replacements since, and a special ceremony in February 2000 planted English oaks to celebrate the Millennium. Oaks Park is still a wonderful place for tree lovers.

To continue the LOOP, turn left soon after entering the park, on a broad drive through ornamental gardens, which narrows to footpath width and keeps near the road for a while. It comes to fencing, with paths leading off in four directions. Keep ahead here, skirting right of an

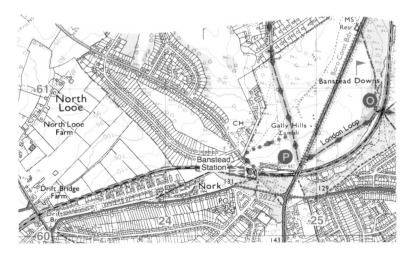

enclosed grass area. The path turns left around the enclosure and comes near the road again before joining a wide track, Fairlawn Road **N**. Turn right and follow it until, just beyond the first house on the left, you bear left into Freedown Lane, a fine old bridleway that passes stables and takes you on to Banstead Downs. On the way, you pass the walls of Her Majesty's Prison, Highdown **28**. On the LOOP, even the prisons sound attractive! At houses, the often-muddy track takes on a metalled surface, leading to a road. Cross and take the track ahead onto Banstead Downs, soon dropping down to cross a railway line, with a fine, open stretch of broom and birch heathland to your right. *At this point, remember that Banstead station up ahead has no Sunday service. On Sundays, it is best to turn right before the railway crossing, to follow the track above the line down to Belmont station, where there is a bus service to Sutton station.*

For Banstead, turn left beyond the railway and follow the main track **O**, ignoring branches to the right. Soon you have the green of a golf course to your left, and waymark posts guide you across a fairway to the noisy A217 road. The helpful posts warn you which way to look for flying golf balls. A golfers' crossing just to your left will get you across the dual carriageway. Enter the drive on the other side, but immediately turn sharp right between little white posts onto a narrow path **P** that soon bears away from the road to cross another fairway and plunge into tangled scrub on the other side. *The LOOP route continues ahead.* But for Banstead station, turn left on a narrow path that comes to yet another fairway, crossing leftwards up to the far top corner. Here a path appears again, leading through scrub to a road, where a left turn will
bring you to the station.

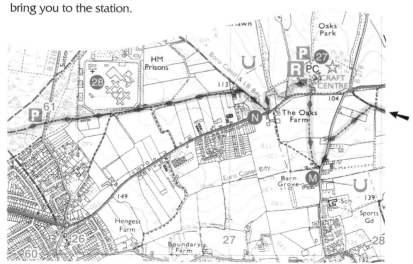

6 BANSTEAD DOWNS TO KINGSTON BRIDGE

10¾ miles (17.5 km) plus ½ mile (0.8 km) of station links. Leave the route at Ewell West station after 3¾ miles (6 km), Malden Manor station after 7 miles (11.25 km) or Berrylands station after 8½ miles (13.7 km).

From Banstead station **A** you have a short walk to join the LOOP route out on Banstead Downs. Take the steps up from platform level to the road, turn left, and some way down go right onto a footpath beside a 'Banstead Road' sign and just before the entry into Cuddington Park estate. Follow the right-hand of two paths out onto the fairway of a golf course, drop down its left-hand edge for a few paces, then walk diagonally right across the fairway to find a track that continues in the scrub beyond. It goes over a crossing track and comes to a junction with another path **B**, where you turn left. *You have joined the LOOP route here.*

Your new path goes over a golfers' track and a metalled drive, and continues ahead as a footpath just right of a green and a bench seat. It keeps its direction, soon following a line of birches down the centre of a broad fairway, going to the right of houses and out to a road junction. Now you have an urban stretch to walk – necessary at present because landowners have not been prepared to make a greener route available. So follow Sandy Lane ahead until you reach Cuddington Way. Turn left here, then first right into Cheyham Way and left in Northey Avenue. You pass a sign proclaiming your entry into Epsom & Ewell, soon after which it is best to cross to the other pavement. Coming to a big roundabout with the modern St Paul's Church on the corner, turn sharp right into Cheam Road, the A232. This is quite an oddity – a main road with service roads to either side and pleasantly green footpaths between them. So cross the service road and take the path beyond until, as you reach a bus shelter, it is time to cross Cheam Road itself to walk down Bramley Avenue, the turning opposite.

At the bottom, a tunnel under a railway line **C** takes you out into green fields again. This is Warren Farm, a 53-acre property given to the Woodland Trust in 1994 after long arguments over its possible fate as a housing development. Cross it via the prominent track leading into the tree belt ahead, over a couple of concrete ways and out to the elegant vistas of Nonsuch Park. The track that heads off rightwards across the open grass leads to Nonsuch Mansion **29**, a Gothic-style house of 1804 with gardens, café and toilets – well worth the diversion if you have time.

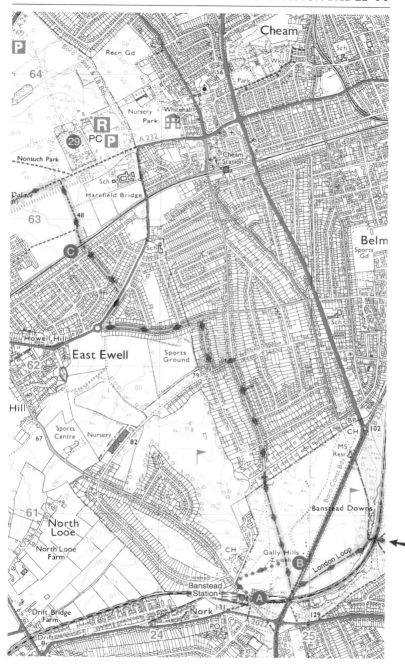

The LOOP goes left along the main drive, content with its wide views over the park, so cleverly screened by tree belts from the suburbia all around. Coming to Castlemaine Lodge, a brief diversion along the drive to the right just beyond brings you to three marker stones which reveal where Henry VIII's exotic palace of Nonsuch once stood **30**. The third stone along is on the site of the entrance gatehouse and it has a plan inset to guide you. The site was excavated in 1959 and the fragments of carved and gilded slate, stone and plasterwork gave some clues to its lavish decoration. Although Henry seems to have devoted his last years to the creation of Nonsuch, he never saw it finished, and Elizabeth I made far more use of it. But in true Henry VIII style, he had the village of Cuddington destroyed to make way for his palace – the excavations revealed the outline of Cuddington church underneath the palace courtyards, and on Warren Farm we were walking the fields once tilled by these medieval villagers. The village, the palace, and all the pageantry of Elizabethan times has departed, leaving nothing but this innocent stretch of grass.

Low brick walls enclose the raised grassy platform on which stood the banqueting hall – all that visibly remains of the Tudor Nonsuch Palace.

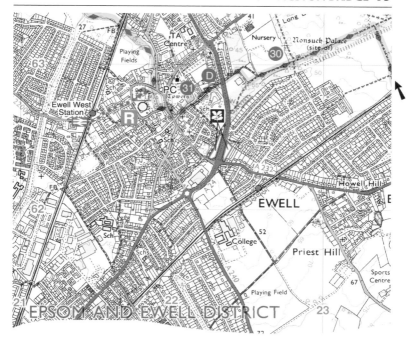

Returning to the LOOP, keep ahead past the lodge on a lesser path, passing a waymark pillar with the number 2 on it. Almost immediately fork right on a simple earthen path that passes pillars 3 and 4. At number 5, turn right, and very soon you are walking beside a roughly rectangular platform with corner bastions, defined by low brick walls. Here, it seems, stood the banqueting hall of Nonsuch. 'Banquet' today suggests a lavish meal, but this was truly a hunting lodge overlooking the deer park, where parties would drop in for the Tudor equivalent of a quick snack. Keep on past these walls and turn left to drop down the field edge to the bottom corner, where steps lead onto a road, the A24. A crossing facility takes you over its two carriageways, then you cross diagonally over a service road and down more steps to a footpath **D** beside houses.

This leads out to a corner of Church Street, where you continue ahead to the shops of Ewell High Street, passing several good buildings on the way. Firstly the early Victorian Ewell Castle, with castellations everywhere you look, then Well House of around 1700. Across the road you could be deceived into thinking that the parish church stands there in the trees, but what you see is only a tower **31** – the rest of the medieval church is gone, replaced by an 1848 version further

Although the 1770s mansion of Bourne Hall, Ewell, has disappeared, its imposing arched gateway still admits us to the grounds.

down in the same churchyard. On the left-hand corner by the shops is the little Watch House with a barred window to one of its doors, where misbehaving Ewell citizens spent the night.

Turn right here and, opposite the white archway entry, cross by the pedestrian island and go through the arch into Bourne Hall Park. *There are toilets here, beyond the crossing.* In the park, walk ahead, but soon bear right on a path beside the lake. To your left, up a grassy slope, a large flying saucer seems to have landed. This is today's

Bourne Hall **32**, a library, local museum and coffee bar, replacing the big mansion, demolished in the 1960s. *As the lake ends, a path on the left will lead you to Ewell West station. If you take it, fork right very soon on a path that follows the walled edge of the gardens, turning right when it meets another path, to exit via a gate in the wall. Outside, turn left beside the wall to a three-way road junction, crossing to take Chessington Road opposite, along to the station.*

This lake and several other ponds nearby form the source springs of the River Hogsmill. Just as you followed the waters of the Cray up from the Thames estuary at the start of the LOOP, so now you return to the Thames at Kingston via another tributary. Walking on beyond the lake, you leave the park and cross the road outside, with a view of Upper Mill over its millpond ahead. Turn right and walk up to the traffic lights, then left on the metalled path **E** towards the mill. The Hogsmill, with its vigorous springs and rapid drop, was excellent for driving flour and gunpowder mills, and Upper Mill is the lone survivor of many, both here and in Kingston. Turn left to the mill frontage, then right on a path that sets off directly in front of it. There are busy little water channels everywhere here, but keep the main flow of the Hogsmill to your right, crossing a little humped bridge, then a flat timber bridge. Coming to a railway embankment, the path uses an ingenious wooden causeway above the Hogsmill to squeeze through the same tunnel. Be sure to duck under a low pipe at the far end!

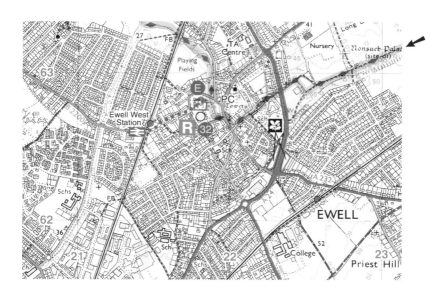

In the open again, go a little way to the right, then over the grass to keep following the river, now just to your left. Keep left of a small fenced-in waterworks enclosure, then cross via a footbridge over the river to walk with it on your right for a while. The Hogsmill is on its best behaviour here, flowing between stone banks. The next footbridge takes you back over again, and once more you are walking over open grass with the river, now much strengthened by tributaries, down to your left. In these watermeadows, with their graceful stands of trees, you catch the occasional glimpse of suburban rooftops to remind you how deeply you are penetrating into urban London. A concrete path crosses the river and starts away rightwards, but ignore it and keep ahead by the river bank. Cross a road via a conveniently placed pedestrian island, and go on along a metalled path, the river to your left and houses to your right. Soon you are on grass again, and the next footbridge marks the point where the biggest tributary, the Bonesgate Stream, adds its waters – a pleasant spot with the open fields of Tolworth Court Farm beyond. Don't cross here, but continue up to the A240, Kingston Road.

You can see the path continuing beyond the traffic **F**, but crossing is hazardous at this point, so go right and cross at the traffic lights, walking back over Worcester Park Avenue and over the Hogsmill to turn right through a wooden barrier onto a riverside path. As a change from rural scenes, at one point this path passes above a go-cart track where kids can enjoy all the thrills of a racing circuit. The path finally exits via another barrier into a drive, where you turn right over the Hogsmill up to a road, with the big Hogsmill Tavern opposite. Their sign shows hogs snuffling by a stream, but in truth the river probably got its name from a miller, name of Hogg!

There is, as yet, no path that continues by the river, and the B284 road to the left is narrow with no pavement or verge, so the LOOP takes a safer route here. Cross the road and go ahead up Cromwell Road, taking the first turning on the left, Grafton Road, to the top of a hill. Fork left here into Royal Avenue, a thoroughfare with a split personality. It becomes a footpath briefly, then an unmade road, then joins a metalled road again – still Royal Avenue. When it turns downhill, keep ahead on a footpath **G** along the top of the slope, dropping to that perilous B284 again, which thankfully has now acquired a pavement. Cross and turn right uphill briefly, then left on a track which passes the church of St John the Baptist, Old Malden **33**.

The church is now an odd, patchwork mixture. You can see medieval flintwork in the chancel, but nave and tower are simple brick from the early 17th century. Not to be left out, the Victorians added their own nave and chancel, requiring the church to be reconsecrated. Malden derives from the Saxon *mael-dun* – a cross on a hill, and here stands the little church on its hill above the Hogsmill, probably the religious site that gave the name to Old Malden.

Through a swing gate beside a five-bar gate, the LOOP turns left and steeply back down to the Hogsmill. *Malden Manor station is nearby. To reach it, go right instead of left on a path that turns down through new housing to a road, where you turn right and very soon left to the station.*

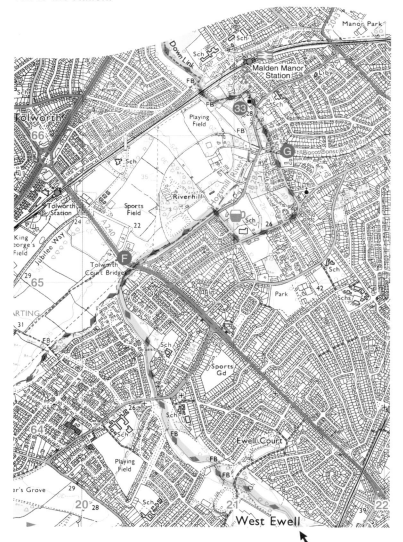

From Ewell Springs, where the river rises, the path by the Hogsmill follows a surprising green corridor, with suburbia to either side.

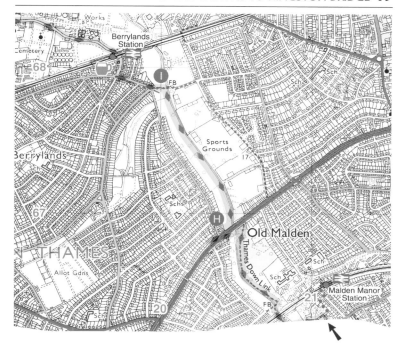

Coming to the river again, don't cross the footbridge but continue with the Hogsmill to your left, following it under a railway bridge and on. Soon a gate, some way up from the river, leads out to the dual carriageway A3, the Malden Way. Turn left to cross the Hogsmill until, coming to shops, you can cross the service road (watching out for two-way traffic), use the pedestrian underpass, then retrace your steps back towards the Hogsmill again. Where the flats end, a gate **H** leads into Hogsmill River Park, and you take the path that drops back to the river bank. The tangled wood across the river here is a nature reserve, and crack willows droop over the water – a last taste of tranquillity before plunging into Kingston.

Follow the Hogsmill now until a footbridge takes you over a side stream. Soon after, you turn left on a crossing path and cycleway **I**, up to a road corner. *Just across the road, a bus stop offers a service into Kingston if you want to skip the urban walking ahead.* Keep ahead on the road, Surbiton Hill Park, to a roundabout with the big Berrylands pub on the corner. Turn right here, down Chiltern Drive to Berrylands station, where trains run to Waterloo. Go ahead under the station name board and through the tunnel beyond to follow Lower Marsh Lane. Once this green way must have been attractive, but today it treats you first to sewage smells wafting over the hedge, then some light industry and a graveyard. Arriving at busy roads, you turn right along Villiers Road, over the Hogsmill and then over the road to take a broad, red-surfaced path on the left **J**, just before an estate of new apartments in two-tone brick. Soon you can hear the rushing of water over a weir, and you come to the charming Swan pub with its Millstream Bar, back by the Hogsmill.

Go left over the river and take the path on the far bank. You cross a second channel, surely a millstream, and go right via a wire-mesh gate to follow a more modest path along the waterside. Coming to a blue girder bridge over the Hogsmill, turn up left to the road, then, a few paces on, go sharp right into Denmark Road. Beyond one group of flats and just before Heron Court, a path on the right **K** takes you back along the Hogsmill, emerging at a busy road junction in the heart of Kingston. Cross via the pedestrian lights almost directly ahead, then turn right to follow the pavement round to a second set of lights, where you cross again and walk ahead into St James's Road. Just before it crosses the Hogsmill, turn left on a riverside path which goes through and even under the complex of Guildhall offices. The biggest block, with the pointed-roof tower over it, is the Guildhall itself.

As the path leads into the High Street, you can see the tops of seven stone columns that surround the Coronation Stone **34**, over to your right. The stone has moved around quite a bit, and now rests in the Guildhall car park, very convenient for the Mayor's Rolls, and whatever conveyances were used by Saxon kings. By tradition seven of them, starting in the year 900 with Edward the Elder, were crowned on this cold block of stone. Further along to the right here is the market place, the bustling heart of Kingston with its stalls overlooked by a cheerfully Italianate market hall of 1840, fronted by a gaudily gilded statue of Queen Anne, rescued from an earlier town hall.

But this stretch of the LOOP must end on the Thames, so cross the High Street, turn right and go over the Hogsmill one more time, via the Clattern Bridge. Just beyond it, go through the little iron gate and look back to discover the three stone arches of a late-12th-century bridge underneath today's road bridge – an amazing survival. A new walkway leads to the Thames entry, from where you can turn right and pass the Gazebo and the Bishop pubs on the way to Kingston Bridge **35**. While bridge-widening work is in progress, take the steps on the right up to road level. *The next LOOP section continues by doubling back over the bridge,* but for Kingston station keep ahead into the pedestrianised shopping area, branching left after passing the Bentall Centre into Fife Road, leading directly to the station.

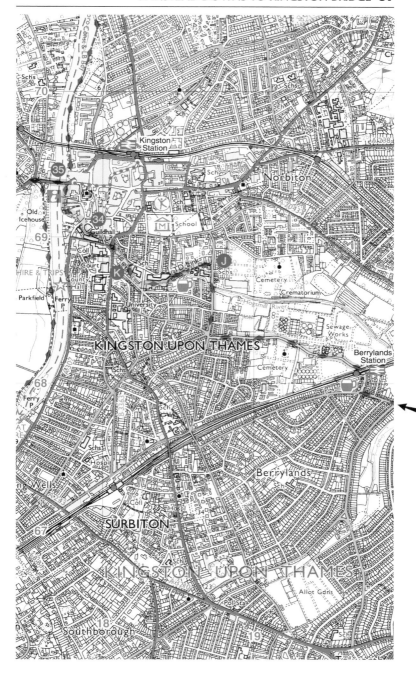

7 KINGSTON BRIDGE TO DONKEY WOOD

9 miles (14.5 km) plus 1 mile (1.6 km) of station links. You can leave the route at Fulwell after 4 miles (6.4 km), or Hanworth Road after 6½ miles (10.5 km).

Finding your way from Kingston station **A** to join the LOOP on Kingston Bridge is easy enough. Your main problem, perhaps, is escaping the lure of all those tempting shops! Keep reminding yourself that you are going for a walk, and set off from the station exit by crossing two sets of pedestrian lights, bearing right to follow the road lined with shops, Fife Road. Soon you will see the Bentall Centre ahead, where you bear left into the pedestrian zone with Kingston's biggest stores around you. Turn right and cross the main street, passing the parish church and turnings to the market place on your left, then follow the footway over the newly widened Kingston Bridge. *You join the LOOP route here.*

Over the Thames on the Hampton Wick side, bear left at the round-about to pass the gates into Hampton Court Home Park, then cross the main road at traffic lights to enter the turning opposite, Church Grove. Coming to the Victorian church, turn left through a narrow iron gate in the brick wall **B** to find that it leads onto an impressive horse-chestnut avenue – one of the entries into Bushy Park. Go through a big iron deer gate and soon leave the stony track to branch right on a broad grass path and thus come out into the open park. Bushy was one of the three parks enclosed by Cardinal Wolsey as part of his Hampton Court estate and given to Henry VIII along with the palace. Now you gaze over an expanse of rough acid grassland, still grazed by deer, with occasional tree plantations to retain its park-like quality.

Ahead, two tracks set off across the tussocky grass. Take the right-hand one, heading straight for the right edge of a small plantation. Through the bracken, it brings you to Leg of Mutton Pond **36** just beyond the trees, where you bear left to cross a low brick bridge over a water channel where it leaves the pond **C**. Once over it, turn left to follow the water channel, soon having to go right to skirt around the bank of a second and odd-shaped pond, Heron Pond. You will come to a criss-cross wooden footbridge. Don't cross this, but keep ahead, walking with another watercourse just to your left to a run of white railings where the water vanishes underground. Bear left here to pass a vast old handpump on a plinth, then keep ahead through the lines of trees to cross the famous Chestnut Drive. This was originally planned to provide a grand approach to William III's new north wing of Hampton

Court Palace. The wing was never built, but the chestnuts mainly survive, a magnificent sight in spring when the huge white blossoms are out. In truth, only the rows lining the drive are chestnuts; the outer rows are limes. *(To the left along the drive is the Diana Fountain, with toilets beyond, by the park boundary.)*

Roots of swamp cypress by the River Longford in Bushy Park.

Walk across the drive through the tree lines and you come to more white railings, where our watercourse emerges again. Now you can see that it flows out of the Woodland Gardens **37** ahead. Keep to the left of the water, and very soon go through an unobtrusive gate in the fence **D**, into the gardens. Turn left now, and follow the path that wanders through the woodland, keeping the waterway always to your right. Looking to the water's edge, you will see the strangest growth around the entire LOOP – the aerial roots of swamp cypress – their jagged stumps pointing skywards like a dentist's nightmare. There are benches here, inviting you to linger by well-tended lawns. Wooden gates take you across a narrow open strip to enter a second woodland garden, guarded by a tiny keeper's hut. This is the Waterhouse Plantation, where the rhododendrons and azaleas really take over – a glorious sight if you choose the right month.

Keep ahead on the main path, forking right at two points to stay near the right-hand edge of the plantation. You come to a little clearing with a pond, a meeting of paths and a cottage, River Lodge, to complete the picture. Bear right here, and take the track **E** just left of the lodge, to walk inside the woods with open parkland to your right. The track ends at a wooden gate into a crossing track. This is Cobblers Walk **38**, with another stirring tale to tell of the struggle to save access to our green spaces. The hero here was Timothy Bennet, shoemaker of Hampton Wick, who established this as a right of way across the park. Detour a few paces to the left along Timothy's path and it gives you a delightful view of the River Longford – source of all the water we have been walking by. The Longford was a remarkable engineering job for its day, ordered by Charles I to bring water 13 miles (20 km) from the Colne to supply his new ornamental lakes and fountains in the palace grounds.

But your route now turns right in Cobblers Walk, through a second gate into the open park. Turn left to follow a path by the fence until it comes up to join a park road near Upper Lodge. You are most likely to see the deer here. Bushy Park supports some 300 in total, the red deer stags recognisable by their rounded antlers with points, the smaller fallow deer bucks by their flattened antlers. Go left along the road for a while, but when it turns left, take the right-hand of two metalled paths ahead, passing a little pond to your left, and leaving the park via the iron deer gate **F** into Laurel Road. Keep to the earth path ahead, cross a main road (the A313 Hampton Road) via pedestrian lights to your left, and keep forward in Kings Road. Take the first left, Connaught Road, and cross another main road, this time the A311. *Fulwell station is just a short way down to your right from here.*

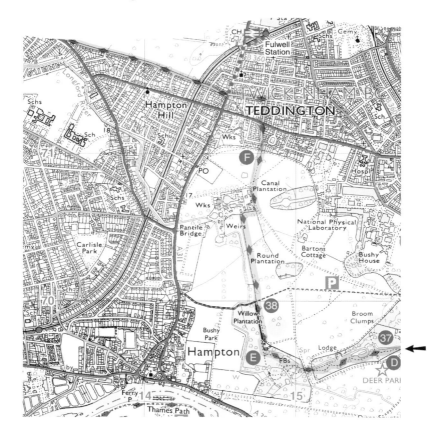

Across the road, continue down Burton's Lane, soon with the greenery of a golf course to your right. When the lane finally meets a main road coming in from the left, turn right on a path **G** between two concrete posts. Bear left, then almost immediately right across the middle of a grass area on a path that leaves a golf driving range to its left, and a clubhouse to its right. Coming to a main road, the A305 Staines Road, turn right, cross at the first island and take the first turning on the left, Court Close Avenue. Very soon turn right into Rivermeads Avenue, then first left into Bye Ways and right at the end into Willow Way. Coming to another busy road, the B358 Hospital Bridge Road, turn left and soon cross over the River Crane. The path we want is below us, so walk on to a gate **H** where you can go sharp left and drop down diagonally over open grass to the riverside. The way goes under another road via a dark, rather spooky causeway beside the Crane, then into Crane Park, where you have a choice between the metalled track or less formal paths by the river.

In Crane Park old millstones lie at the foot of the Shot Tower, reminders of the gunpowder industry that once thrived here.

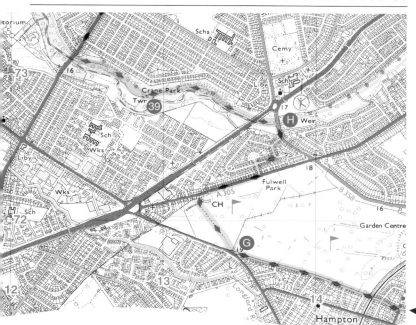

Soon you will notice high earth banks around you, and you come to the gaunt brick tower usually known as the Shot Tower **39**. Here, from the 16th century on, were gunpowder mills that used the waters of the Crane to drive their millwheels. The powder was ground in small wooden sheds enclosed by those banks to retain the force of the all-too-frequent explosions. If you worked in the sheds, it was doubtless reassuring to know that your remains would not be plastered all over Hounslow! Experts insist that the tower is not high enough for the manufacture of lead shot, so it must have served either as a watchtower or possibly a water tower. Today it is an interpretation centre for the Island Nature Reserve, reached via the wooden footbridge over a mill sluice at its foot. A path circuits the island and its many habitats if you have time to spare.

Otherwise, continue via the paths near the Crane which eventually rejoin the metalled way and come up to the A314 Hanworth Road. Ahead now, the Crane reaches Hounslow Heath via a tunnel under the old Feltham Marshalling Yard site, but the LOOP must get there via a road diversion. Turn right along the A314, passing shops and a pub, and crossing to the other pavement at the first opportunity. *(You will pass bus stops with services to Heathrow, Hounslow and Kingston.)*

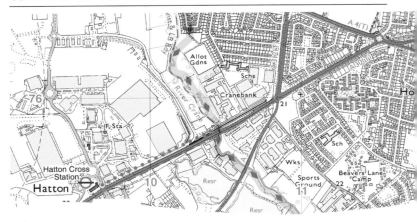

Cross over railway lines, then, reaching the green space of a recreation ground, turn left through a gap in the fence **I** and along the left-hand edge of the grass. A path goes through a tree belt, over a stile and ahead into the open vistas of Hounslow Heath. This amazing survival still retains a wild character, even while tower blocks define its edges. Across the rough grassland are scattered patches of gorse and broom, all untamed, and you can still conjure up images of days when highwaymen and footpads gave the heath its evil reputation, and the coach road across was lined with rotting bodies on gibbets, swinging and rattling their chains in the harsh wind. I hope I'm not putting you off!

Take the most prominent path ahead onto the open heath, which soon forks gently left. Some way on, shortly before coming to a lonely little bench, fork left on a grassy track that aims directly for a distant church spire against a background of office blocks. This track keeps straight on over several crossing ways, then comes to a junction with a track that clearly follows the boundary of the open heath, with a belt of trees just beyond and the trimmed grass of a golf course visible through the trees. Turn right on this track **J**, a bridleway, keeping near the tree-lined edge of the heath, until you come to an open area with several paths meeting. Turn left here on a narrow path **K** that squeezes between two sawn-off tree stumps and enters a narrow gulley. Turn left on the track along the bottom of the gulley, then, when it ends, keep on in the same direction over a green, soon joining a track that drops to cross a bridge over a millstream, then almost immediately a second bridge over the wider Crane. Turn right after crossing the Crane, and walk with the river just to your right as it follows the edge of Brazil Mill Woods. Soon you can see a little single-span bridge ahead, Baber Bridge. Just before it, the path turns up left to reach the A315 Staines Road. *To your left here are shops, a café and the Crown & Sceptre pub.*

To continue, cross the A315 by the lights just to the left, then return to the Crane and go left through a green barrier into Donkey Wood. The path crosses a sluice, then goes via a footbridge over a millrace **40**. Here were more gunpowder works, and from the drop over the weir you can still judge the power that drove the mill, of which only a few walls of ruined masonry survive. The water is the Duke of Northumberland's River, cut around 1520 to serve these mills, and others in Bedfont and Isleworth. While the river powered the millwheels, the willow and alder growing along the Crane provided charcoal, an essential ingredient of gunpowder.

The path wanders on past more high banks, which shielded the working sheds, then crosses a footbridge and continues beside the high fence of the Causeway Nature Reserve. It goes under another road, squeezing along the bank between the Crane and factory fences, then up to a busy dual-carriageway road, the A30. *The next LOOP section continues by the Crane, and you reach it by walking a few paces to the left, carefully using a gap provided to cross the A30.*

But for Hatton Cross station just turn left along the path beside the A30, pass the first traffic lights, then very soon, at the second set of lights, cross rightwards to the station.

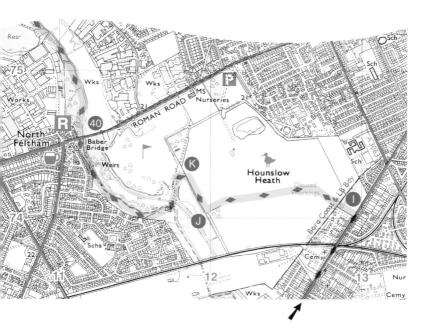

8 DONKEY WOOD TO UXBRIDGE LOCK

10½ miles (17 km) plus 1 mile (1.7 km) of station links. You can leave the route at Hayes & Harlington station after 4 miles (6.5 km), or West Drayton after 7 miles (11 km).

You start this LOOP section accompanied by the roar of jet engines, and end it with the sleepy thump-thump of a canal narrow boat – sounds that are truly centuries apart. Leave Hatton Cross station **A** by the Great South West Road exit, turn left, and cross a road at traffic lights. Stride on along the path beside the main road, the A30, admiring the mighty jumbo jets parked outside the British Airways hangers to your left, then, coming to a concrete wall that conceals the Piccadilly Line trains, go left of it on the service road. *The LOOP route itself has come up from Donkey Wood and made a rather hazardous crossing of the A30 at this point.*

Soon, the service road crosses the River Crane and you can turn left through an elaborate barrier **B** to follow a path through Crane Bank Water Meadows. Keep to the gravel path, past occasional benches and glimpses of the meandering, reed-filled Crane. It takes you through a second barrier where you turn left, then right at a path junction, and left again to leave the meadows via a third barrier, between houses. Coming thus into a suburban road, Waye Avenue, turn left and follow it around several bends until it reaches a main road, the A4 Bath Road. Just to your left a subway takes you under the traffic; it is so extravagantly decorated with animals, fishes and all manner of creature, there is simply no room for grafitti! Having climbed the steps on the other side, cross the modest High Street and walk on down the Bath Road to cross the balustraded Cranford Bridge **41**. Here was the ford that gave Cranford its name, and the bridge still proudly carries the shield of the now-departed County of Middlesex.

Where the railings end, go right under the arch **C** into the open grass of Berkeley Meadows. You can see the Crane to your right, flowing on under a single-arch brick bridge, and at the very end of the grass strip you come into a lane and turn right. Very soon, hidden away behind a road barrier, you will find a narrow path **D** heading leftwards into the woods. Little streams are everywhere, and you cross a couple of plank footbridges, soon bearing left with the Crane itself to your right. Now you are following a broad, grassy track along the edge of Cranford Park, with glimpses of its church away in the trees to your left. Coming to a footbridge over the Crane, use it as a marker

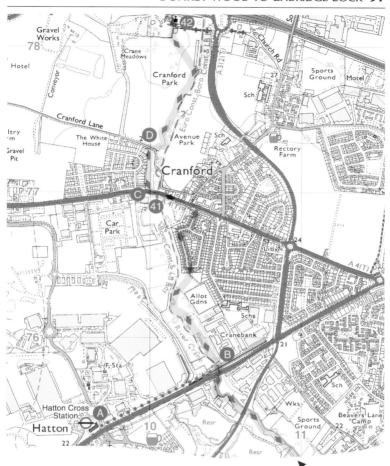

and bear left over the open grass towards the church. Leaving a children's play area to your right, you will reach the corner of the 18th-
century ha-ha, a sunken wall and ditch that separated the gardens of
the Earl of Berkeley's mansion from his 1000-acre park.

This estate was bought by the Berkeleys in 1618, but the house
became ruinous after their departure in 1918, and was finally demolished in 1939. What little remains you will see in a moment, but first
walk across the car park and turn left in front of the church. St Dunstan's
42 is a delightful mix of materials – a 15th-century tower of flint with a
later top storey of brick, and a whole nave of brick rebuilt after a fire in
1710 by the Dowager Duchess of Berkeley. On the east end they firmly

With its graceful curve, little Bull's Bridge is a typical canal crossing, taking the towpath over the Paddington branch of the Grand Union.

claimed ownership by placing the Berkeley arms in stone, while inside, as befits an estate church, are all the family monuments, not only to the Berkeleys but to Sir Roger Aston, who sold them the estate.

Through a gate you come to the stable block, a red-brick range looking over a cobbled yard with a strange, solid block of hedge at its centre. Here was the imposing headquarters of the Berkeley Hunt, but today not even the clock works. Turn right through the further archway of the stables, then under the M4 motorway via St Dunstan's Subway, and turn right again on the other side. St Dunstan was not the patron saint of underpasses – this way was simply provided to give parishioners access to their church.

The track soon leaves the motorway to bear left into the young woodland of Dog Kennel Covert. Follow the bridleway, and soon the thunder of the M4 gives way to the twitter of songbirds. You come out into a broad grass strip, at the end of which turn right, then soon left on an old hedged track, Watersplash Lane. When it wanders into trees, keep ahead to the very end of the grass, through a gate and up a drive to a road alongside the Crane pub. Turn right here, cross at the traffic lights, then go over the River Crane to reach a big roundabout, where you bear left on the footpath and cycle path beside the dual carriageway A312. Road and paths all climb purposefully, and you soon realise that you are crossing the Grand Union Canal. Once over the canal, a ramped way **E** begins to drop down to the towpath, via twists and turns that leave you wondering whether it is ever going to get there. Once eventually on firm earth, the gleam of white catching your eye to the left is Bull's Bridge **43**, well worth a brief diversion. The fingerpost by the bridge tells it all – directing you to Birmingham, Brentford or Paddington. Here, the main line of the Grand Union keeps ahead to join the Thames at Brentford, while the branch to Paddington Basin departs under the white arch. The towpath of the old canal now provides an excellent long-distance walk, and we turn and follow it for a while towards Birmingham.

Walk under the A312, then under a rail bridge to a further road bridge. *At this point you can reach nearby Hayes & Harlington station by turning up the brick steps just before the road bridge, turning left and left again to cross the canal, with the Old Crown pub on the corner opposite, to pass a roundabout and climb the slope to the station.* But continuing along the towpath, just beyond the bridge you pass an iron milepost of the G.J.C. Co., proclaiming: 'Braunston 87 miles'. So what company was this, and why should we want to know

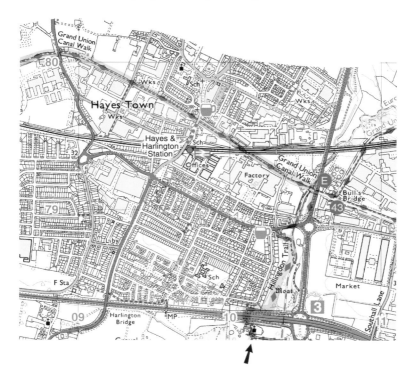

the distance to remote Braunston in Northamptonshire? The Grand Junction Canal was the original title of the ambitious 93-mile navigation approved by a 1793 Act of Parliament to link Braunston on the Oxford Canal with Brentford. Created through the sweat of thousands of navvies and the genius of engineer William Jessop, it linked the industry and coalfields of burgeoning Birmingham with London. It only took on the 'Union' title in 1929 when several canals amalgamated. Keen-eyed walkers may notice that the original canal bridges are numbered down from Braunston – you will soon pass under number 199.

After two more road bridges, the second a simple, old-style brick arch with iron corner bars to protect towlines from chaffing, you will be walking beside a reedy dock inlet behind railings on your right. You have reached Stockley Park **44**, and the LOOP does some exploring here. Turn in through the steel kissing gate **F** just beyond the inlet and follow the gravel path up to a road, with fountains and cascades to your right, and hi-tech offices to both sides. Coming into the open, you can begin to marvel at the scale of this newly created landscape. Before 1985 this was derelict and abandoned land – old brickfields used for rubbish dumping. Today, 250 acres (101 hectares) have been transformed into a golf course and country park, funded by the handsome business park that takes the rest of the site. A staggering three million cubic metres of refuse were moved to form the hills you now scale, with over 140 thousand trees and shrubs planted to establish the wooded areas. Topsoil was a problem, and the designers Arup Associates tell with relish how one and a half million worms were brought in to activate a soil-forming process.

Cross the road and fork left along a footpath **G** lined with young trees. It crosses the broader horseride, but soon after this you fork right towards the big grandstand-like building that is the golf clubhouse (*it has a first-floor bar and cafeteria with magnificent views, open to the public*). Coming to a road, bear left to leave the clubhouse to your right, then having passed it fork immediately right on another gravel path. For a while you have views over the golf course to one of the two viewpoint hills, then the path goes through young woodland planting and curves up to the strange single pylon of the bridge that links the two halves of Stockley Park. Cross the bridge and take the broad track ahead, leaving it very soon to branch over the grass up to the second viewpoint knoll, with its amazing views across the Colne Valley. Be sure to drop down again smartly, for your route takes a left fork **H** just beneath the knoll, dropping to fork left again, soon with a horseride to its left and floodlit playing fields to its right.

Where the track swings left towards office blocks, drop down right to leave Stockley Park via a gate into Horton Road.

Across the road, a further park area has not yet been opened to the public, so you must turn right and endure some local industry until the third turning on the left, Horton Bridge Road, takes you back to the canal. On the way, you pass the Brickmakers Arms, reminder of the trade that once thrived here. Back on the towpath again, you pass a run of great timber stores on the far bank, further reminders of how valuable the canals were in moving bulk materials like this. *At the next bridge, with a swan motif in brickwork, you can reach West Drayton station, shops and pubs, by turning up the cobbled slope to the right, and taking the road over the canal.*

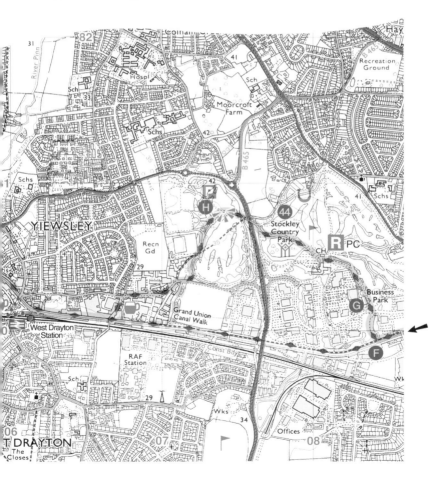

Continuing, and just beyond another milepost reading 'Braunston 82 miles', you come to a criss-cross girder bridge **45** over the canal. You have reached Cowley Peachy Junction, and we cross this old bridge to follow the Slough Arm of the canal for a while. Despite its present setting of rural tranquillity, this 5-mile branch was virtually the last canal to be built in this country. Back in 1882 it was needed to meet London's growing demand for bricks from the brickfields around Langley. Very soon a cast-iron aqueduct takes canal and towpath over the Frays River, an intriguing manoeuvre! The Grand Union shares this valley with several water courses, including the River Colne, and millers insisted that it be built *higher*, so that they would not lose their precious water supply. Hence the need for an occasional aqueduct.

Coming to a steel footbridge, pass under it, then turn sharply left up the bank to cross the canal. You will be circling round a granite obelisk here **46**, carrying the arms of the City of London. This is a coal tax

By Little Britain Lakes the River Colne presents an idyllic picture, looking towards the ford where Packet Boat Lane crosses.

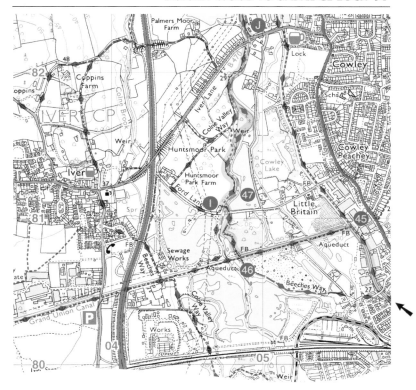

marker, one of many to be seen on the main trading approaches to London, warning that you are due to pay tax on the coal you are bringing in. The tax was introduced in 1667 to help rebuild the city after the Great Fire, and it is odd that the LOOP meets so few of these posts on its circuit. Over the bridge, the track runs through wild woodland and soon you meet the River Colne, to your left, for the first time. You emerge unexpectedly at Little Britain Lakes **47**, a series of delightful, willow-hung waters, once gravel pits – a spot to linger in for a while.

Walk ahead and cross the Colne by footbridge **I**, turning right along a path that has the Colne to its right and the fields of Huntsmoor Park to its left. It crosses three little sidestreams and joins a more prominent track, still by the Colne. After passing a pretty weir, you come to a road, forking right to take steps up the bank. Turn right to cross the river, going over to the pavement side, then where the bridge railings end, turn sharply left onto a footpath **J** that continues by the Colne. In contrast to the paths you have enjoyed so

From Uxbridge Lock the LOOP follows the Grand Union Canal towpath north into rural country, with colourful narrow boats moored by the bank.

far, this one is narrow, often overgrown, near to slithering into the river – a path in dire need of some loving care. Persevere – it has some charming stretches. Eventually it leaves the river to follow a side channel, joining a track that soon becomes a road, Longbridge Way, through a small industrial estate. At a crossing road keep ahead down Culvert Lane to rejoin the Grand Union Canal towpath, turning left along it to pass the General Elliott pub. Now the office blocks of Uxbridge loom ahead, the remnants of the little market town lost beneath them.

At the second road bridge, Uxbridge Lock **48** lies just ahead, *and that is the way the LOOP goes.* But for Uxbridge station turn up steps on the left immediately after passing under the bridge, into the Swan & Bottle car park, then up more steps to the A4020 Oxford Road. Go left again to cross the canal, then over Sanderston Road at traffic lights to bear left up Uxbridge High Street. Through the pedestrianised shopping area, the station is on your left.

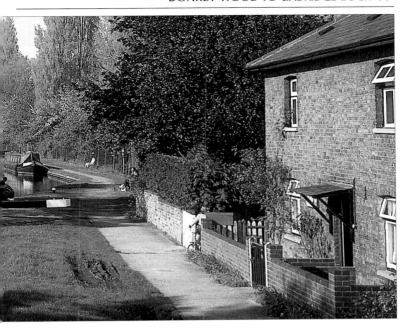

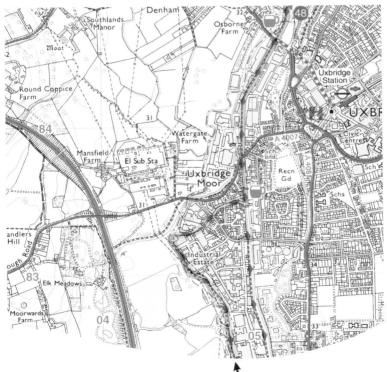

9 UXBRIDGE LOCK TO MOOR PARK

9¼ miles (15 km) plus 1 mile (1.5 km) of station links. You can leave the route at Harefield West after 5¼ miles (8.5 km).

Uxbridge reminds you of its past as soon as you step out of the station **A** into the town centre. There, across the concourse, is the long Market House of 1788, its open ground floor now occupied by shops. Uxbridge was indeed one of the most important market towns of Middlesex, and today's brash shopping precinct retains the lively bustle, if nothing else. The parish church is hidden behind the Market House, giving the odd impression of having been chopped off at an angle by its self-important commercial neighbour.

Turn right through the pedestrianised area, all that remains of the winding High Street. Once this was the Oxford Road, and Uxbridge provided the first stop out of London for the Oxford coaches – as witness the several surviving inns and yards. Cross Harefield Road and continue downhill over the Frays River. In passing, note, across the road, the mellow brick frontage and Jacobean gabled end of the Crown and Treaty pub **49**. Here on the road to Oxford was the logical place for the Commissioners of Charles I and Parliament to meet in 1645 to try to negotiate a treaty. After 20 days of debate they parted, with no treaty agreed, and around 1800 what remained of their meeting house was converted into the inn you see today.

Cross the Grand Union Canal, then turn immediately right down steps to the Swan and Bottle car park, and via further steps to the canal towpath, *turning left to join the LOOP route*. At Uxbridge Lock **48**, just ahead, cross the canal and continue past the lock cottage. This is a popular spot for traditional narrow boats to gather, and you might be lucky enough to see a couple going through the lock together. These locks were built wide enough for two narrow boats to squeeze in, side by side, and in the days of commercial traffic they were worked in pairs in this way. The powered boat would tow the unpowered 'butty' behind. When today you see these boats converted, with twee names like 'Little Gypsy' or 'Narrow Escape', remember that the earlier canalboat families had to live in the two tiny cabins aft.

Across the canal, the modern buildings of Kings Mill stand on a site where flour has been milled for a thousand years, with the waters of the River Colne providing the power. Shortly before you walk under the A40 road bridge, the Colne can be seen sweeping in to join the

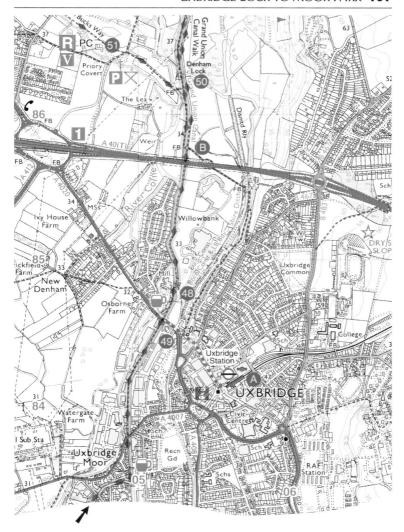

canal for a brief union. At the next bridge **B**, a traditional canal arch, cross and walk on towards the little white cottage of Denham Lock **50**. As the thunder of traffic fades away, you begin to enjoy the Grand Union in its rural peace. *By way of a diversion, just before the lock, a path to your left crosses the Colne and leads into Denham Country Park. If you walk ahead through a gate, on the gravel track across Misbourne Meadows, the Colne Valley Park Visitor Centre 51 with its exhibition, toilets and coffee shop, etc, is just ½ mile (1 km) away.*

With London left behind, the Grand Union Canal towpath enters a scene of rural peace, heading towards Denham Lock.

But the LOOP continues past Denham Lock. This is the deepest lock on the canal, which has to take a great leap up here to clear the Frays River, which crosses beneath, just beyond the lock. *On the lawn betwixt canal and river, as delectable a spot as you will ever find, you can relax in Fran's Tea Garden, open every day except Monday but closing at 3.30 pm in winter.*

Some way beyond the lock, you cross the canal via bridge number 182, then go immediately left on a path **C** over a ditch, to turn left onto a track that has the broad waters of Frays Valley Nature Reserve **52** to its right. Gravel was quarried here, as elsewhere along the Colne Valley, but now the pits have returned, quite gloriously, to a natural state. The track bears left under a railway viaduct, a majestic great skew bridge of dark brick. Now the canal is back beside you, and an even more vast expanse of water to your right, with a sailing club to its far side. The track turns right to go between the lake and a marina crammed with rows of colourful narrow boats. Where the track bears left, keep ahead on an unsurfaced path **D**, turning left when it meets a crossing path. Through a green gate you are on a broad metalled track again, but a short way down it a gate on the left **E** leads to a delectable woodland path with lake, lawns and picnic tables tempting you to linger. This leads out through barriers to a road, where you turn left and soon find yourself crossing the canal again. *Ahead is the Horse and Barge pub,* but to regain the towpath go down steps on the left to double back under the bridge and on past Wide Water Lock.

Soon, a fine sweep of buttercup meadow drops down to Black Jack's Lock **53**. Here the Victorian mill and an earlier fishing lodge stand on an island between two waterways, and you cross the mill-race by footbridge. Around another couple of bends, the canal comes to what was the Fisheries Inn, now renamed the Minnow, and the spot long known as Copper Mill **54**. The big mills here were converted in the early 19th century from paper to the making of copper sheeting. Its prime use was the protection of wooden ships from the dreaded marine worm, but legend has it that the copper orb on the dome of St Paul's Cathedral also came from here. You can still see water streaming through the millrace, and the big mill-owner's house that tells of past prosperity. But the mills have gone.

Cross the narrow canal bridge, watching out for light-controlled one-way traffic, and turn left into Summerhouse Lane, just beyond the mill house. *To leave the walk here, continue up the hill, soon coming to the turn-round point and stop for the U9 bus, running into Uxbridge from Monday to Saturday. On Sundays keep on up to Harefield village and turn right in the High Street for another bus service, the 331.*

Along Summerhouse Lane, take the first turning on the right **F**, signed 'Hillingdon Trail'. At first you are following a road past houses, then a rough track ahead, then an enclosed path climbing up through Park Wood to the left of the entrance to Parkwood Kennels. Coming to a road, turn left and cross to the pavement side, soon passing a building that was clearly a pub and still has the 'Plough' sign outside, even though it now proclaims itself to be a children's learning centre. Past the next bungalow, turn right into a short roadway **G**, crossing a stile at its end, to maintain the same direction over a meadow on a clear little path to a footbridge with stiles in the hedge on the far side. Continue with a hedge to your left and a vista of rolling fields ahead, over a stile and into a dip, where another stile and footbridge awaits you. Cross these and continue uphill beside the remnant of an old field boundary to your left. At the top, climb one more stile and follow the hedge on until, at the entrance to Feldways Farm, you join their track and follow it to a road, the Harefield Road.

Turn right uphill, with an eye on the traffic – this busy lane has no footway. Reaching the car park of the Rose & Crown, turn left onto an enclosed footpath **H**. Where the enclosed stretch ends, go slightly right downhill to a field corner, through a gap in the hedge and on with a wood to your right. Soon you cross a shallow dip with a broad and tempting grass track in it. Resist the temptation and keep ahead outside the wood until, shortly before the field ends, you can turn

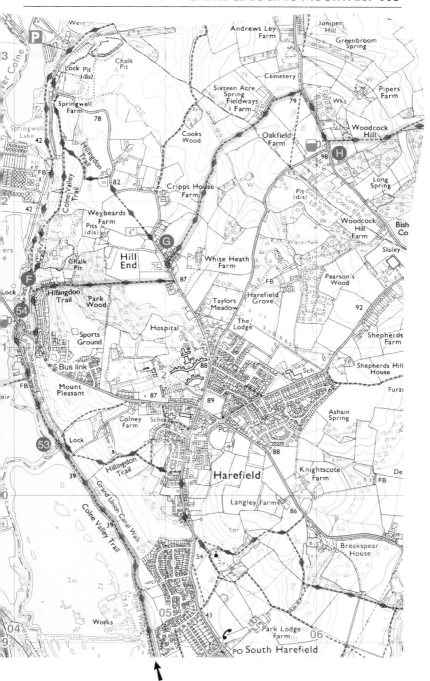

right up the bank and over a wooden barrier **I** onto a path through the woods. Now you are in Bishop's Wood Country Park **55**, a string of once-coppiced woodlands, now renowned for the richness of their plant life.

The path keeps on through the woods, eventually going through a gate to join a wider track, where you bear left and continue. Before long this new track dips into a hollow with a stream at the bottom. Go left here, just before the stream **J**, on a modest path that follows the stream, then crosses it and continues, keeping near the woodland edge to your left. On leaving a patch of conifers for more deciduous trees, turn right and come very soon to a crossing track. Turn left now, following the white arrows along a horseride towards Batchworth Heath. Beneath an electricity pylon turn left, then just before a second pylon the horseride, sometimes rather muddy, nears a road. It leaves the trees, coming out to the open grass and pond of Batchworth Heath **56**, with the A404 road ahead, and over it the more welcome sight of Ye Olde Greene Man pub.

Cross the busy main road with care, turn right and cross Batchworth Lane to follow the pavement of the main road past the more modest Prince of Wales pub. A little way beyond the pub, just before a street light, turn left onto a narrow path **K**, surfaced with paving slabs. As you turn, look across the A404 to a little white post by the roadside. This is a 'coal-post', one of many erected in Victorian times to mark the boundary within which you had to pay duty on coal and other items you were

Just a scattering of houses and an inn stand around the open grass of Batchworth Heath, with a reedy pond to picnic by.

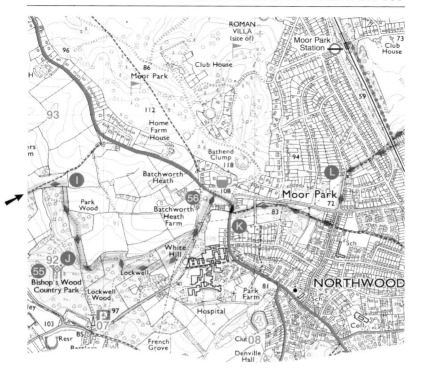

bringing into London. Indeed, this odd paved way is a rarity – a boundary path which once divided Middlesex from Hertfordshire. And you may soon note another odd feature. Over a crossing road, the path continues on raw earth, but in weather-worn piles along it are the slabs obviously intended to pave it. Why wasn't the job finished? It is as though some ancient 'beating the bounds' ceremony got this far, then gave up!

The boundary path crosses open ground and a woodland patch, then runs between house gardens to a road, Kewferry Road. Turn left here, cross over Batchworth Lane and continue in the road opposite. Pass Heathside Road on the right, then when your road swings left, turn right onto an enclosed footpath **L**. Cross another road, going half left to find the path continuing, hidden in hedges. Cross one further road and go under the railway on a narrow road ahead, turning left immediately onto a footpath. *Coming out to rough, open ground, the LOOP continues as a grass track heading half right.* But for Moor Park station keep ahead on the path into a woodland belt, following whichever path keeps nearest to the railway line to your left. When the woodland path meets Sandy Lodge Lane, turn left into the station subway.

10 MOOR PARK TO ELSTREE

11½ miles (18.5 km) plus ½ mile (0.8 km) of station link. You can leave the route at Hatch End station after 4¾ miles (7.6 km) or Stanmore after 8¾ miles (14 km).

Moor Park **A** is a confusing station – it tries hard to start you off in the wrong direction. As you pass through the ticket barriers, the obvious exit is up ahead. But no: you turn sharp right to the subway that doubles back, signed to 'Sandy Lodge'. Having passed all the platforms again, it takes you up steps to emerge at the back entrance. Turn immediately right to follow a path through woodland, where many waymarks strive to keep walkers near the railway and out of Sandy Lodge Golf Course, up the bank to your left. The path leaves its woodland and continues along the right-hand edge of rough, open land to reach a sturdy metal barrier by houses. *You join the LOOP route here.*

Don't go through the barrier, but turn sharp left to follow a broad grass track **B**, guided by helpful wooden posts with 'FP' painted on them. After a while, at a post, the waymarked track bears slightly left to go under electricity lines. At a crossing track it turns half left to enter the golf course, where it immediately turns right to follow frequent yellow 'FP' markers over several fairways. Keeping a wary eye open for golfers, you reach the far side of the course via a path that enters a small wood and emerges on Sandy Lodge Lane. There is a fine view here, north over the Colne Valley; this is your last glimpse of the river as its canal companion heads north for Birmingham and we go east along London's edge.

Turn right on the path beside the lane, down to a main road, the A4125 Hampermill Lane. Cross with care, and go leftwards a little to find a hidden path **C** between squeeze posts. It climbs with houses to the left, then soon bears right into open fields. Turn up left now to follow the left-hand tree line, then when it dips and ends, keep ahead towards distant houses. This is a fine expanse of public land, and it's a good feeling to stride off over the open grass. Over a rise, a little fenced-off play area comes into view. Before reaching it, bear right to a gap in the houses where a gate leads across grass to a road, Ashburnham Drive. Turn right here and, coming to a T-junction, turn left and take the first road on the right, Nairn Green. At its end, keep ahead on a path **D** into Oxhey Woods **57**.

A short way in, turn left along the bottom of the woodland slope, then, where another path joins from the left, bear right over a sleeper footbridge and take the broad track that climbs through the trees.

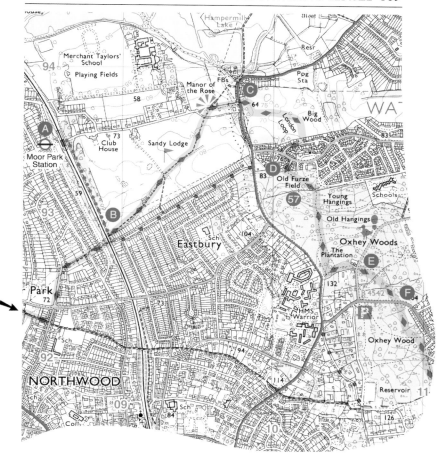

Keep ahead, ignoring crossing tracks, and at the top you will begin to hear the sounds of road traffic to your right. Eventually the track divides, one branch obviously joining the road. Fork left here – there is a little sawn-out tree trunk seat to mark the spot – and very soon you will see a house through the trees ahead. Your track goes right of the house, out to a lane beside the drive to Oxhey Wood Lodge.

Cross the lane and continue on a footpath beyond a steel barrier **E**, keeping ahead over a crossing track to reach a busier road at a convenient crossing island. Another barrier across the road leads down steps to a path **F** heading slightly leftwards. It comes to a clearing in the woods, where you keep left and join a broad forestry track for a while. Where the track bends away right, leave it for a footpath that keeps ahead and drops

Pinnerwood House, glimpsed over its garden pond, was the home of the author Edward Bulwer Lytton in the 1830s.

to cross two tiny streams, with houses in sight to your left. With the path rising again, you begin to sense that you are nearing the edge of the woods, and at a broad cross-track you turn left. It drops gently through Nanscot Wood, then ends rather abruptly at some houses, where a path on the right leads out to the open fields of Pinnerwood Farm.

Walk along the top of the fields now, a hedge to your left, until, passing the first of two close-together kissing gates **G**, you will stop to absorb the view south over the farm. Much of London is in view, with the spire-topped rise of Harrow on the Hill prominent in the middle distance. Drop down over the rough meadow grass towards the buildings of Pinnerwood Farm, following a hedge to your right. A kissing gate leads into the farm area, where you turn right on their track and immediately take a narrowly enclosed and signed path on the left, which skirts around the farmyard to emerge beside the Victorian farmhouse. Pause to admire its intricately moulded bargeboards, then walk down the concrete farm drive. On your right is the early-18th-century Pinnerwood House **58**, and your second view of it over its pond gives a charming cameo impression of a moated farmhouse – don't miss it.

The concrete drive turns left, and a short way on, a footpath **H** sets off on the left, over a stile and along a field edge with trees to your left. At the field corner turn and follow the hedge down to a kissing gate and foot-bridge. Cross and skirt rightwards round another field edge, soon walking with house gardens to your right. *The second stile on the right, just before the field corner, will take you to Hatch End station. It leads into Grimsdyke Road, which you follow leftwards, bearing left down to a main road. Turn left here and pass shops and a pub to fork left into the station forecourt.*

The LOOP crosses a further stile in the corner of the field to a path **I** into scrub woodland. There are several paths wandering leftward, but all lead to an enclosed path with a playing-field fence, then house gardens to one side, and open farm fields to the other. When the houses end, the path turns briefly right, then left over rough grass to a stile. From here, go ahead over the field, aiming for a distant electricity pylon. Beneath it, go through a rickety farm gate and on by a right-hand fence, soon with new housing to your left, up to Little Oxhey Lane. Go over to the foot-way and follow the road rightwards, over a railway and up to a busy road junction. Cross here at a pedestrian island by traffic lights to take the footpath ahead **J**, signed 'To Grimsdyke'. Restoration work may bring

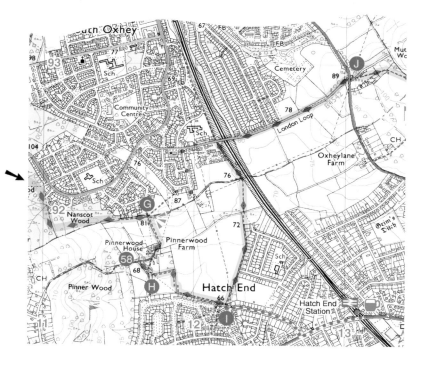

minor changes to the footpath route here, but essentially it climbs a strip of rough ground to a kissing gate on the right, leading onto Grim's Dyke Golf Course. Once on the course, skirt left around a green, then walk up the hill, with trees to your left, to a cottage at the top. Go right of the cottage, then left to join a track leading onwards. On the right, watch out for a panel telling that the ancient earthwork called Grim's Dyke **59** crosses here. Once it could be traced for miles, but this is the only substantial stretch remaining where it can be seen as a ditch and bank. It probably marked a boundary, and excavations suggest a date of around 100 AD.

Opposite the panel stone, take a path **K** on the left into the woods. It runs just inside the woodland with open fields to the left, then comes to a small pond with a vast array of telecom bowls looming beyond like a flock of roosting spaceships. Turn right here on a path that crosses Grim's Ditch and joins the drive to the telecom station, where you turn right again. Just as you think you are entering a road, go left on a path that crosses two plank bridges over ponds, keeping just below the road for a while. But then you are squeezing through banks of rhododendron to pass a bigger lake **60**, darkly overgrown with a lost quality about it – a melancholy spot. And truly, it has a tale to tell. These were the grounds of Grimsdyke House, designed by Norman Shaw in 1872 in his extravagant Tudor style, which in 1890 was bought by W.S. Gilbert, literary half of the renowned Gilbert and Sullivan team. Gilbert lovingly tended his country estate, and once declared that he would like to die on a summer's day in his own garden. On a summer afternoon in 1911 his wish was abruptly granted when he drowned here in the lake under mysterious circumstances – one version has it that he was teaching two young guests to swim. Old mossy stone slabs suggest some forgotten island feature – four pillars are all that remains of a summer house. A sad spot to remember a man who gave us so much laughter.

Where the lake ends, bear right up a bank and turn left again to follow a path along its top. The humps and bumps all around you here cannot be blamed on Grim. You are on Harrow Weald, where, in the 19th century, the locals exercised their right to quarry the gravel capping on their high common. Their efforts, combined with the nearby brick kilns of Old Redding, devastated the area. The tree cover you walk through today is a mix of young birch woodland that has flourished since the commoners departed, and the specimen trees of Gilbert's estate (you may spot several majestic sequoia).

The path you are following turns right to join the road at Old Redding, opposite a car park and picnic field with spectacular views south. Walking left along the road, you pass a pub with the intriguing name 'The Case is

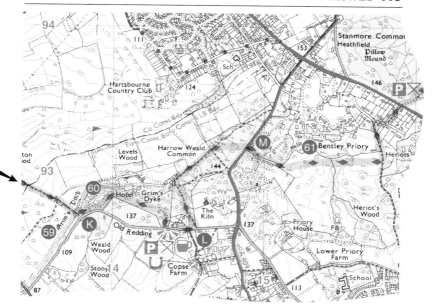

Altered'. Most pubs with this name trace it to a licencing decision by local magistrates, but this one prefers the Spanish version – a corruption of *casa alta*, or high house. High it certainly is, and its name board shows soldiers of the Peninsular War period gleefully spotting a pub.

Beyond the pub, opposite a pedestrian island, go left through a gate **L** onto a broad track into the woods. Follow it right up to houses on the woodland edge, then turn right on a track that keeps along the edge. Eventually the open fields end, and soon after there are 'Bentley Priory' signs pointing you rightwards through the trees to a flight of steps up to a main road, the A409. Cross and go through a five-bar gate **M** opposite, onto a concrete path that leads out to Bentley Priory Open Space. No directions are needed here – just keep to the concrete. To the left above you runs a double barbed-wire fence with security lights, guard-dog warning notices, even a pillbox – quite regardless of the rural tranquillity all around. Bentley Priory **61** is still Air Force property, proud of the part it played as Fighter Command Headquarters in the Battle of Britain. You will see little of the massively Victorian house exterior from the path, except perhaps a distant glimpse of a rather Italianate tower.

When you arrive at a big fingerpost and information boards, turn left on a track that runs beside the security fence up to a road, Priory Drive. Turn right and very soon left to reach a main road, the A4140.

Cross at the island on the left to take Warren Lane opposite. A short way down, cross into a car park, where, at the bottom, on the right beside a walk information board, a path **N** sets off. It parallels the lane, crosses a drive, then returns to the lane by the corner of a cricket field. Take the path opposite, which goes between two ponds, then bears left to keep near a field full of rugby pitches. It brings you to a metalled path, which you follow leftwards, turning with it to enter a road. Don't follow the road, but bear left immediately along the edge of an open grass area, keeping left to reach the first of the ponds on Stanmore Little Common **62**. *Out of sight here, but just to your right, is the Vine pub.* The ponds are sometimes called Caesar's Ponds, going by the theory that the Romans dug them. With their nearby rustic cottages, they make a memorable scene.

The attractive walk option down to Stanmore station starts here. Turn left along the bank of the first pond, keeping ahead to a road junction, where you cross and go down Dennis Lane opposite. Some way down, just before double traffic islands, go left through a kissing gate into Stanmore Country Park. The track ahead crosses an open strip, then bears right in the woods beyond, dropping to a plank footbridge. Cross this and bear left uphill again. At a meeting of paths take the middle of three, then a right fork, and just beyond a little electricity substation bear right via a kissing gate to the top of Kerry Avenue, leading straight down to the station.

The LOOP continues by bearing up left before the first pond ends, to skirt round above the second pond. Coming to the road, walk ahead, then left into Warren Lane. At a road junction take the lane furthest to the right, passing a straggly fragment of Stanmore Common, then houses, to arrive at hospital gates. Go left here, then immediately right through a smaller gate, to a narrow path **O** which runs beside the hospital fence. Where the fence turns away, drop down the bank to keep ahead on a farm track with views north as you descend the slope off the Harrow Weald ridge. The track turns right and very soon you leave it for a grassy track **P** on the left, leading over an earth bridge into an open meadow. The path is invisible here in the tussocky grass, but it goes ahead over the rise on a line that gradually approaches the motorway on the right. Soon you can aim for a road bridge going under it and, coming nearer, a stile leads into a concrete drive beside a fenced pumping station, and thus into the road.

Turn right under the motorway, bearing right to circuit the roundabout, then crossing at the island to take Elstree Road, opposite. One day, perhaps, we will be able to avoid this road walk and cross the fields instead, but for the moment follow the pavement, soon with the open water of Aldenham Country Park **63** to your left. Just beyond the Fishery Inn, cross to a stile opposite **Q** to enter the country park. Turn right along their Lakeside Walk, passing a dinghy sailing club and coming to an open area where tracks meet. The LOOP goes right here, on a rough drive along the far side, but it is worth walking ahead briefly on the path along the dam for its views over the water. The reservoir was built around 1795 to allay the concerns of mill-owners that our old friend the Grand Junction Canal would lower the levels of nearby rivers

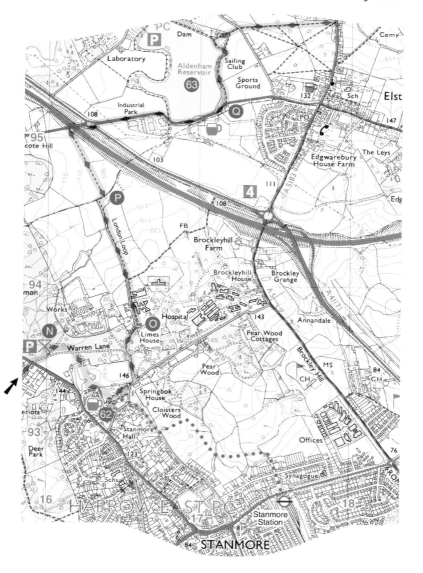

and take their trade away. French prisoners of war were brought in, and contributed just the sort of reluctant effort you would expect. For two years they dug up everything in sight – clay, gravel, rubbish, even vegetation – and dumped it across the stream to make a dam that has leaked and shifted ever since. *Vive le revolution!* The dam is now safely concreted, *and across it are toilets and the Clockhouse kiosk for refreshments, open every day in summer.*

The rough drive takes the LOOP up to a road, where you cross to a stile opposite. The path runs ahead with a fence to its left, and a characteristically English view opening up to Elstree Church spire on its hilltop, over the fields. Through a rickety iron kissing gate, the path keeps its direction over open grass to a simple bar stile onto Watling Street **64**, the great Roman highway to the north. Cross with care – the chariots run faster these days – and take Allum Lane, almost opposite. Very soon cross to a stile **R** on the left, and a path that goes ahead for a while, then curves right with a ditch to its left. When the ditch turns away, keep ahead via an earth bridge over another ditch, then up the field towards a line of poplars on the skyline. A stile takes you onto a golf course.

There are several rights of way here, and this route keeps you on clear tracks. Turn left along the edge of the course to find a track **S** leading into a woodland belt. In the woods, fork right on a track that comes into the open again and swings right to join a wider track towards a little shelter with a picnic table under it. Take the fainter track left of the shelter, crossing a little footbridge on the left shortly before reaching trees, then over a stile into the rough grass of Parkfield. Walk now with the trees to your right until, coming to a metalled path, you turn right **T** to follow it through the woods and up to a road, Allum Lane again. Turn left, cross at the first island and take the pleasantly green path beside the road towards Elstree & Borehamwood station. *Where Deacons Hill Road turns off to the right, the LOOP continues that way.* But for the station keep ahead, over the railway bridge and down the steps on the right.

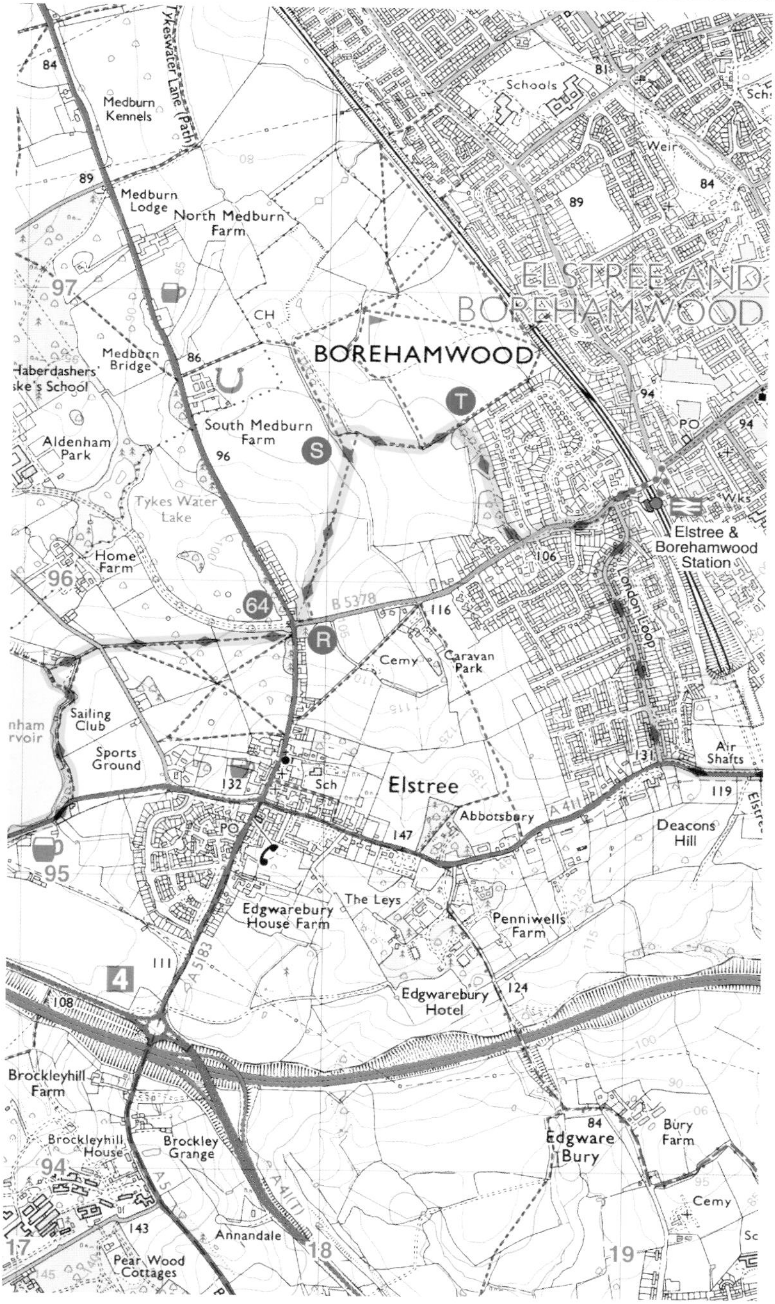

Tykeswater Lane (Path)
Medburn Kennels
Medburn Lodge
North Medburn Farm
CH
BOREHAMWOOD
ELSTREE AND BOREHAMWOOD
Schools
Weir
Medburn Bridge
Haberdashers' Aske's School
Aldenham Park
South Medburn Farm
Tykes Water Lake
Home Farm
B 5378
Cemy
Caravan Park
Elstree & Borehamwood Station
Wks
PO
London Loop
Sailing Club
Sports Ground
Sch
Elstree
Abbotsbury
A 411
Air Shafts
Deacons Hill
The Leys
Edgwarebury House Farm
Penniwells Farm
A5183
Edgwarebury Hotel
Brockleyhill Farm
Brockleyhill House
Brockley Grange
A5
A 41(T)
Annandale
Pear Wood Cottages
Edgware Bury
Bury Farm
Cemy

11 ELSTREE TO COCKFOSTERS

10½ miles (17 km). You can leave the route at High Barnet station after 7 miles (11 km).

It has to be admitted: this section contains too much road walking. Right from the station, it should be possible to climb a green strip, running pleasantly up to the heights of Deacons Hill, but this route has not yet been negotiated. Then, coming to the dual carriageway A1, we find that it ruthlessly cuts off one country park from another, and we have to make a long detour to find a safe crossing. But enough griping – there are delights ahead too, as we set off from Elstree & Borehamwood station **A**. From the exit walk ahead, then up steps on the left to road level, turning left again to cross over the railway. Just beyond the big garage, turn left up Deacons Hill Road, *joining the LOOP route at this point.*

It's a steep pull up, but at the top turn left along Barnet Lane, the A411. The road dips and rises, and near the top you will spot gaps in the left-hand hedge **B** that enable you to take to open ground (although the LOOP officially keeps to the pavement). There are good views north, and paths that keep near the road, soon following along a narrower strip of scrub land, fenced off from farm fields. Eventually the path rejoins the road opposite a little red pillar box. Cross here, and take the path **C** on the right, just a short way on, immediately before Bay's Hill Cottage.

You cross a stile and drop down towards the old oak woodlands of Scratchwood **65**, entering them past a log barrier, so enormous it could keep elephants out! In the woods turn left on a crossing track, which drops and joins another track, still keeping near the woodland edge to the left. It crosses an open area, with an elegant stand of pines by the path, beyond. Once, both Scratchwood and its country-park neighbour, Moat Mount **66**, were part of one big shooting estate, and the conifer belts encouraged the game birds to fly high.

Coming to a bigger expanse of open grass via a kissing gate, you can see the Scratchwood café and toilets up ahead. But the LOOP turns right here **D**, down the edge of the open space past picnic benches, to take the right-hand of two paths into scrub woodland. The path drops, bears left, then climbs again to reach the A1 road via a squeeze barrier. Now the roadside tramp begins, and you can curse the designers who ignore our humble need to cross roads like this. Rightwards we can eventually use a pedestrian underpass to cross and return on the other side to

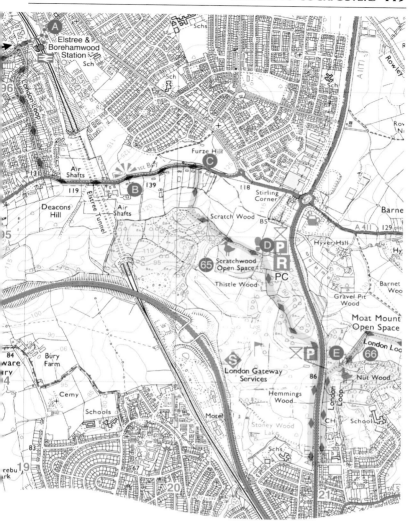

reach the entrance to Moat Mount Open Space. Turn in here, grateful to escape from the thunder of traffic, and walk ahead on the broad tarmac path, keeping ahead when it turns left, on a lesser track into the woods. A short way in, fork left on a footpath **E** which drops down a neat flight of steps with handrails, then follows a little stream up through the woods. Tall trees soar above us here, a reminder that these were once the grounds of Moat Mount House, landscaped in the 19th century with some exotic plantings, including Wellingtonia.

The path joins another and bears right, now as a fenced way over farm fields. Keep to the clear main path, with several kissing gates to take you over farm tracks, then in a dip you may notice the merest trickle of water to both sides. Here is the source of the Dollis Brook **67**, and you will see more of this stream. A little way on at a dividing of ways **F**, bear right and keep along the woodland edge to a road, Hendon Wood Lane.

Turn right here, crossing to the footway. Round a right-hand bend, at the top of a rise and just beyond a sports-club entry, turn left through a kissing gate **G** into Totteridge Fields. The path drops by the left-hand hedge through two fields, turning left at the bottom, along the lower edge of a football field until, halfway along, a plank bridge and gate take you into meadows again, bearing left to follow the hedge. Through yet another kissing gate you are on an enclosed path for a while. Now you can just relax and stroll through the fields, content to keep the hedge, and soon the infant Dollis Brook as well, somewhere reassuringly to your left. This stretch by the brook has the lingering feel of an ancient hay-meadow landscape. The remains of massive old Hertfordshire hedgerows divide lush, flower-speckled fields. Rural bliss ends when a big three-way footpath sign points you across the Dollis Brook via a gate and a decidedly urban footbridge, and the first houses of Barnet are suddenly just a field away.

Now you follow the other bank of the brook, along a grass strip with houses to your left. At a crossing track, look for a modest little stile to the right, to continue, soon joining a tarmac path on the

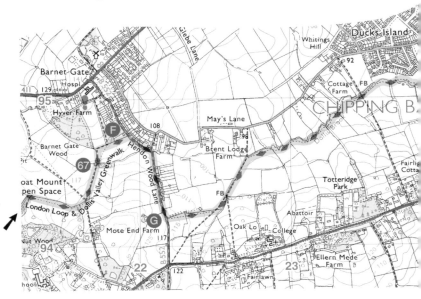

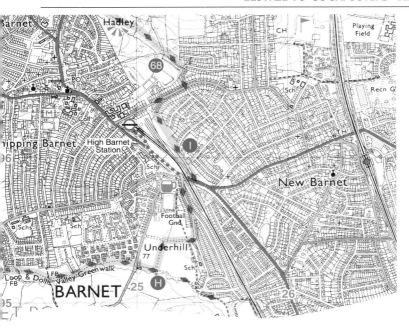

grassy shoulder above the brook. Approaching a road, Barnet Lane, fork right into it, cross and turn in beside the Table Tennis Centre. Beyond the car park, go through a hedge gap and turn left almost immediately on a track **H** through the middle of playing fields. At a junction of tracks turn right up to a road, where you turn left. This soon becomes Fairfield Way, leading up to the Old Red Lion pub on the A1000 main road. *A left turn here in front of the pub will take you up the hill and over a pedestrian crossing to High Barnet station.*

The LOOP turns right under the railway bridge to cross the main road at pedestrian lights and go sharply left up Potters Lane. Just before reaching houses on the left, turn left down the bank **I** into a field of lush grass. A faint path keeps to the right edge, dropping to join a little tarmac path with bungalows to its right. This leads out to a triangle of green, where you turn right and walk down Meadway. Near the foot of the slope, turn left into Burnside Close and, where it turns right and ends, continue on a footpath. When you come to the bottom of another road, go left via a kissing gate into King George's Fields **68**. This bracing hillside of open fields and dense old hedgerows was acquired as open space in the early 1930s to celebrate the reign of George V. Walk ahead on the main path, which crosses a stream, then climbs the brow of the hill with views opening up behind you, Londonwards.

From Moat Mount the path drops into the gentle vale where the Dollis Brook ris

ws deep into London to join the River Brent.

Coming up to a road, you are on the edge of Hadley Green. Here, at the highest point along the Great North Road, is the likely location for the decisive Battle of Barnet on Easter Sunday 1471, when Warwick the Kingmaker was slain and his cause lost in the mist. Cross and take the path **J** heading right, along the edge of the green. The first big house you pass, with a charming bell turret over its stable block, is Hadley House **69**, the one-time manor house. Then come several 18th-century cottages, one of them Livingstone Cottage, where the famous explorer lived briefly in the 1850s on returning from his first African trip. *The remaining village pub, the King William IV, is down the main road here called Hadley Highstone, which runs along the further side of the green, so to reach it you would fork left between two ponds.*

The LOOP bears right as the green ends, on the road past the church. On the corner stand Sir Roger Wilbraham's Almshouses, a low run of mellow brick, founded here in 1612 for 'six decayed housekeepers'. Would today's residents behind those six little doors appreciate that description, one wonders? The best-known feature of the church projects from the tall stair turret attached to the tower – the ancient iron beacon sometimes called the Armada Beacon, but more likely to have been set there by the monks of Hadley (the village was owned by the Monastery of Walden, Essex, through the Middle Ages) to guide travellers over the wilds of Enfield Chase. And indeed, as you go through the white gates, you are venturing into Chase country.

Here was once a great royal hunting forest, stretching out to Potters Bar, with few residents except some 3,000 deer. Queen Elizabeth and other sovereigns hunted here, but fashions changed and Enfield Chase

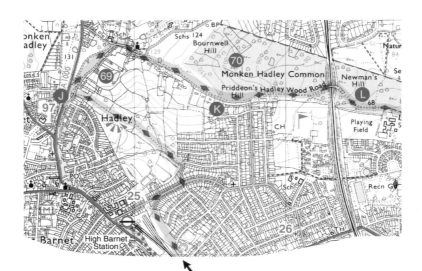

became a neglected wilderness. George III finally gave in to demands and in 1777 an Act of Enclosure saw the Chase parcelled off. Some was sold, but Hadley folk claimed grazing rights and managed to get 240 acres (97 hectares) for their common **70**.

So, from here to Cockfosters, you are traversing Hadley Common. Follow the path beside the common road for a while until, just beyond another big mansion, Hadley Hurst, you can cross and plunge into the woods **K**. Very soon a woodland path crosses and you turn right to keep near the road. The path eventually rejoins the road, now a much quieter lane, Bakers Hill, just leading to a modest car park. Beyond a car barrier the track continues over railway lines, then forking right as a sunken lane **L** through young beech woods. Over a clearing and into woods again, the track keeps near the common edge to its right until, in a dip, it crosses a stream via a pompous little four-pillared bridge. Just beyond, it is well worth diverting left over a plank footbridge and up the bank for a surprise view over Beech Hill Lake **71**. This was created around 1880 by Charles Jack, as a feature in the grounds of his Beech Hill House, and locals still call it 'Jack's Lake'.

The track rises away from the stream, soon with houses to its right, then joins Games Road. You pass traces of another of the white gates, this one leading you off Hadley Common, then the Cock & Dragon pub to your right. *From here, Trent Park, with its toilets and café, is just ahead over the main road.* But the LOOP turns right beyond the pub, into Chalk Lane, forking left immediately, then turning left at a church to follow the lane up to the A111 road. Cockfosters station is almost opposite, and a pedestrian underpass to your right leads into it.

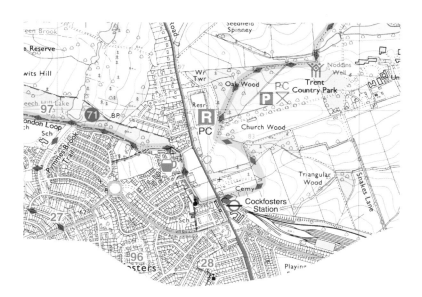

12 Cockfosters to Enfield Lock

8½ miles (13.7 km) plus ¼ mile (0.4 km) of station link. You can leave the route at Gordon Hill station after 5½ miles (8.8 km).

You've seen Cockfosters as the destination on the front of those nifty little Piccadilly Line trains for years, without ever realising that the place actually exists! Yet here you are, stepping straight out of the station into the rolling green countryside of the LOOP. The 'fosters' in the name is probably a corruption of 'foresters', and indeed the country you are about to explore was once a royal hunting forest – Enfield Chase.

From the station ticket hall **A**, take the steps up to Cockfosters Road, and you are instantly on the LOOP route. On the pavement go right briefly, then right again across an area speckled with little yellow posts, to take a path to the left of the station car park entrance. A narrow grass strip runs between the car park and a cemetery, with a path that leads out into open fields. Once in the open, turn left on a grass path **B** that soon enters a tree belt and bears right. Coming to a crossing path in the wood, turn left, soon to bear right and cross a muddy little stream to emerge on open grass again. Bear right to follow the edge of the grass, and join the main drive into Trent Park. Turn right here, then fork left at an obelisk **72** to reach their café and toilets.

Looking back over the Salmon's Brook Valley and Enfield Chase.

Take the track just to the right of the café, left of a Country Park board, to follow it through pleasant mixed woodland until, with a strip of meadow grass in sight through the trees ahead, the track bears right and soon comes out into the open park. At a broader crossing track, turn left to cross a stream, with a lake just to your right. At another meeting of ways, bear left uphill. From this spot you can just glimpse the house of Trent Park **73** across the lake, and before your track enters the trees again at the top of its climb, it is well worth a pause to survey the sweep of fine parkland behind you. When Enfield Chase was parcelled off, George III gave 200 acres (81 hectares) here to his favourite physician, Dr Richard Jebb, as a thank-you gesture for saving the life of his brother, the Duke of Gloucester, at Trento in the Tyrol. Subsequent owners, including millionaire Sir Phillip Sassoon, enlarged the estate, the house and its gardens. The house has seen many uses, including an interrogation centre for enemy airmen in World War II, and is now part of the Middlesex University campus. Although formalised to some degree as a country estate, this vista of groves and greensward is the nearest you will get to the ancient character of the Chase.

Soon after entering the trees, fork left **C** off the main track. When this woodland way approaches green fields on the edge of the park,

bear right on a log-edged path to a road. Looking left along the woodland edge from the kissing gate, you can see the tall obelisk **74** erected
in 1702, more, one suspects, as a garden feature than to celebrate anything of significance. A 'keyhole' cut through the woods provides a
clear sightline to the house. Go left along the road verge for a while,
then cross to a kissing gate and a path **D** that drops into the gentle valley of Salmon's Brook. These further stretches of Chase country became
enclosed farms, and somehow they forgot to provide us with footpaths. The welcome path you now follow is known locally as the Jubilee
Path, because it was sponsored by Enfield Preservation Society and
opened in the Queen's Jubilee year, 1977.

A three-way finger sign greets you on reaching the valley floor, and
you turn right towards The Ridgeway. Eventually the path takes a footbridge over Salmon's Brook and climbs away, while our route continues
via a stile **E**, on a newly opened path by permission of the Enfield Chase
Estate. It keeps beside the brook along the bottom of several big fields,
each rising gently to a cluster of houses on the skyline, with the whimsi-
cal name of Botany Bay **75**. This little settlement grew up on the
Ridgeway road after the forest enclosures in a location so lonely, at the
heart of the old Chase, that some wit likened it to that remote spot on
the far side of the world. After four fields, the path turns up towards The
Ridgeway until, nearing the road, it goes right via a kissing gate into a little memorial plantation, Brooke Wood. It meanders up through young
trees, crosses a stile, and follows the top of a lush meadow for a while
before joining the road. Cross to the footway and go right, towards the
Royal Chase Hotel (which has a public bar). Just beyond the hotel, turn

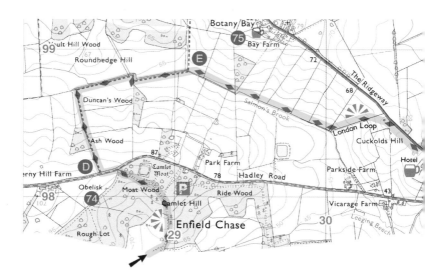

left down the Rectory Farm drive **F**. Follow the drive through the farm, then over a little stream. Note it well – this is the Turkey Brook **76** that rises near Potters Bar and drains much of the Chase country, and we will be following it doggedly until it joins the River Lea.

After passing under a railway bridge, the drive comes to a crossing track, where you turn right, past a vehicle barrier. The track becomes metalled and soon, just beyond a strange, boarded-up factory, you can take a woodland path on the right **G** into Hilly Fields Park. Coming to a tiny clearing where several paths meet, fork left, then soon left again, on a path that emerges at the top of an open field. Walk along the top, then right on a metalled path on its far side, descending to a footbridge over the Turkey Brook, here putting on its prettiest face for this charming park. Cross the brook and fork left to follow beside it. *For Gordon Hill station take the path ahead instead, turning left to follow beside Cooks Hole Road, then right at the crossroads up Cedar Road, and second left up Rendlesham Road.* Coming to a second footbridge over the brook, the LOOP turns up right, briefly, on the metalled path, to turn left again at the top, dropping to the Clay Hill road opposite the welcome Rose & Crown pub.

Cross and take the path ahead, just right of the pub, keeping open grass to your right and the Turkey Brook to your left. The path climbs a bank with traces of an old watercourse to either side. This, confusingly, was the old channel of the New River **77**. Far from 'new', this artificial cut was created in the early 1600s from Chadwell Springs, near Ware, 40 miles down to Islington, to bring fresh water into London. Originally it followed the contours, but in the 1850s this stretch above Enfield was straightened out, and here you are crossing one of the redundant loops.

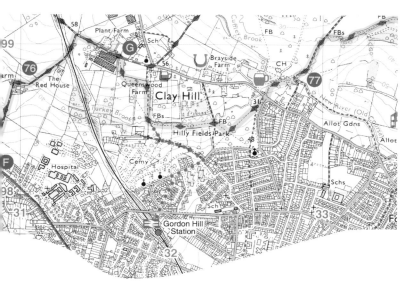

Keep ahead, ignoring all turnings and using the Turkey Brook, on your left, as your guide. Passing a barrier with a tall fingerpost above it, keep ahead towards Forty Hall, forking left, with the open grass of Whitewebbs Park now visible through the trees and over the brook to your left. Soon there are rhododendrons lining the path and a long, dark pond to your right. This was probably the fishpond of Elsynge Hall, a fashionable address in Elizabethan times. The site of the old house is uncertain, and Forty Hall, built in the 1630s, looks over the estate from a much higher location. The house **78**, its gardens, café, toilets, etc are well worth a diversion, and you reach them by turning right as soon as the fishponds end to follow the lime avenue. Forty Hall was designed by Inigo Jones for Sir Nicholas Raynton, Lord Mayor of London. You see it first reflected in its own lake, then circuit round to explore the terraces and walled gardens, nicely maintained by Enfield Council, returning to the lakeside to admire the magnificent Inigo Jones gateway to the stables.

Meanwhile, the LOOP continues by the Turkey Brook until, approaching a road, you cross it via a wooden footbridge **H** beside the more substantial brick of Maidens Bridge. Joining the road, turn back rightwards to cross the bridge (watch out for the traffic lights), and very soon go left, by bollards, onto a metalled path. It climbs a bank between high

Dropping into Hilly Fields Park, the LOOP crosses this footbridge over the infant Turkey Brook before following it to join the River Lea.

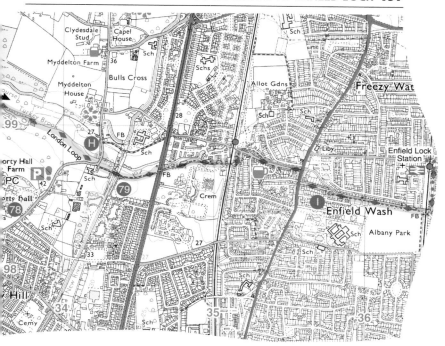

fences and this, believe it or not, is the New River **79**. It has obligingly dived underground at this point, to allow our Turkey Brook to cross.

Now the LOOP has to find a way across the Lea Valley sprawl, so do not expect rural bliss for a while. The path crosses scrubland, then over a main road by footbridge, and determinedly on – its last greenery provided by a crematorium garden. It joins a road, which squeezes under a low railway bridge and comes to houses, where you turn left, then right in Turkey Street (*the station of that name is just to your left*). Clue-spotters will note that they are passing the Turkey pub and, sure enough, there's the Turkey Brook flowing along, just across the road. Coming up to the busy A1010, use the pedestrian facility to cross and go right in the main road a short way, then left into St Stephens Road. Just after it turns right, go left on a metalled path **I** to keep on in the same direction. Soon, our old friend the Turkey Brook turns up by our side again, with the bare grass of Albany Park to the right. As you cross a railway line by footbridge, you can see Enfield Lock station to your left. *Now the LOOP continues by the brook to Enfield Lock itself*, but to end this section take the bridge over the brook and continue down the road ahead, turning left at the bottom, with the Railway Inn on the corner.

13 ENFIELD LOCK TO CHIGWELL

8 miles (12.9 km) plus ½ mile (0.8 km) of station links. You can leave the route at Chingford station after 4½ miles (7.2 km).

Geologically, this makes an eventful day. It starts by crossing the Lea Valley, rich market-gardening country, then climbs over the gravel ridge of Epping Forest to the fertile Roding Valley beyond. First though, it should be explained that Enfield Lock is not actually at the station of that name, but away on the Lee Navigation. So, if you have arrived from the London direction, turn right from the station exit **A**, over the level crossing and first right into Bradley Road. This road ends at the Turkey Brook, now confined within grim steel walls, its surviving greenery providing a refuge for litter rather than wildlife. *You join the LOOP route here.*

Don't cross the water channel, but turn left to follow it on a wide metalled path. It crosses a minor road, then a main road via a ramped footbridge of impressive length. From its top, your eyes move longingly to the vision of green hills ahead – the Sewardstone country beyond the Lea. When the path ends at a road, you have found Enfield Lock **80**. Along the navigation you can glimpse a terrace of workers' cottages, and beyond the lockhouse of 1889 stand foursquare buildings that cannot quite hide their industrial past. Here was the Royal Smallarms Factory **81**, given this formal title in 1854 when a reluctant government decided that those new-fangled rifles really were going to replace the smooth-bore muskets the British Army had got by with for centuries. The first machinery came from America, but soon the factory

A traditional narrow boat edges into Enfield Lock on the Lee Navigation.

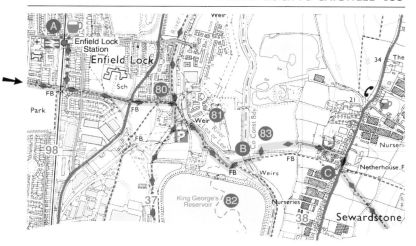

was producing better designs of its own, and the army fought through the Boer War and two World Wars with the rifle that proudly linked the two names associated with this spot – the Lee Enfield.

Walk ahead over the Lee Navigation, then drop down to its tow-path on the right. This is your briefest of brief encounters with the Lea Valley Walk. It starts at the river's source at Luton, and if you followed it southwards you would join the Thames Path at Limehouse Basin. But coming soon to the Swan and Pike Pool on your left, a spot with lawns and benches to linger at, you leave the towpath and go left across a car park and over a bus turning circle to a footpath beyond, signed to Sewardstone. It follows a channel of the Lea to its left, swings away to cross another channel, then returns to the same bank. Eventually you cross the Lea channel via a massive concrete bridge, then fork right across the grass to a new footbridge **B** over a flood-relief channel – fancy steelwork in stark contrast to its older companion. Those delectable Sewardstone hills are much nearer now, and to your right, the long grass bank conceals the vast King George's Reservoir **82**.

Now go half left to a gate into Sewardstone Marsh Nature Reserve **83**. Four grass paths set off from just inside the gate, but yours goes ahead, a broad path that bends right, then left through lush growth with gleams of water to either side. The path becomes concrete, then leaves via a kissing gate into the bottom of a road, Godwin Close. This leads up to the A112 road, where you turn right. The Royal Oak pub here has now gone mauve and aquired the trendy name of 'Freddies', but our footpath still sets off opposite it. Go leftwards over a stile **C**, then immediately right over a second stile and half left up the field, aiming for a small hut on the far side. A stile behind the hut (close up you see that it is a cattle byre) leads onto a cinder track, which you follow ahead towards a tree-clad hill. The track bears right, then climbs up to the trees, but just before it reaches them go right over a stile. Through a narrow tree belt, the path crosses a second stile, then keeps climbing with the hilltop trees to its left. Two more stiles take the path over another cinder track, and it is time to take a breather and look back over the waters of the Lea Valley below you. The two vast reservoirs, King George's first, then the William Girling, supply over a quarter of London's water. They supply other needs too, and as many as 30,000 gulls have been counted on the William Girling.

In the field beyond the cinder track, the path may be invisible. It climbs over the rise of the hill, keeping near the right-hand field edge. When the far side of the field comes into view, aim for a stile a short way in from the right-hand corner. It takes you over the cinder track again, to a stile opposite **D**, on a short path that very soon meets another and turns left with it. The rather boggy land you are on here is Sewardstone Green, an outlying parcel of Epping Forest – once grazing land but now much encroached by scrub. The path leads to a farm track where you turn right to join the nearby road, Daws Hill. On the corner is a vision of bygone times – a perfect little weatherboarded Essex farmstead **84**, viewed over its pond. Nothing about Carrolls Farm would ever dream of lining up. The gables are perversely different, one from another, the windows fall where they please, and the front door refuses to acknowledge anything as boring as a centre line.

Turn left on the road. Paths venture into the opposite verge, where an informal bridleway runs near the road, but 'informal' means often waterlogged. Best keep to Daws Hill until you can turn right into the drive to Gilwell Park **85**. Follow the drive, or its grass verge, to the top, where signs remind you that this is the international centre for the Scout movement. Directions to 'Resource Centre' and 'Campers Car Park' suggest that even Baden Powell's concept has moved with the times! Turn left, following the sign to Sewardstone Lane, then take the green way, Gilwell Lane, that keeps ahead beyond the vehicle barrier. After a while the old lane begins to drop and, halfway down the slope, look for a narrow path **E** leaving to the left by a waymark post. This path, sometimes rather overgrown, drops into an open hollow. If you prefer, soon after starting out along Gilwell Lane, you can leave it for the open Yates Meadow, just to its left, to follow the meadow edge down to a hedge gap leading to the same open hollow. Yates Meadow is 'buffer land' bought by the Corporation of London to protect the environment of Epping Forest.

Cross the little bridge over a stream at the centre of the hollow, then take the track ahead up the open slope towards the trees of Hawk Wood. At the top, turn left on a crossing track **F** and enjoy the wood – a taste of the forest with tall oak and hornbeam, and much evidence of old pollarding. The horseride keeps level, with a golf course just above it to the right. It comes out on Bury Road, where you cross and turn right, either along the pavement or the horseride that follows the road just inside the trees beyond. Coming out to the open grass of Chingford Plain, keep ahead, either on or near the road. The Willow Café by the roadside is open from 7 am to 3 pm every day. *For Chingford station, keep ahead to a road junction, bearing right over Forest Approach and up Station Road into the shops, where a pedestrian island takes you over to the bus and train stations.*

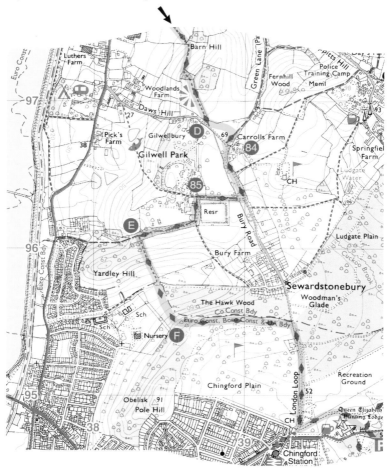

The LOOP continues by taking a surfaced track on the left **G** onto Chingford Plain, just beyond the café. Where it ends at a 'crossroads', take the grass path that bears right up the hill towards the trees. The first little white building you meet beyond the trees is known as Queen Elizabeth's Hunting Lodge **86**. Dating from the early 16th century, this is a rare example of a 'standing' used to view the hunt in the forest below. To get a better idea of this function, imagine the two upper floors completely open – just the timber frame and no plaster work or windows that you see today. The building is L-shaped and the shorter wing is one great staircase of solid oak – supporting the legend that Elizabeth was in the habit of riding her horse up it. The white, weatherboarded house further along is Butler's Retreat, a restaurant now, but one that retains a welcome custom of serving honest mugs of tea from a side window.

Hawk Wood gives you a brief experience of the true Epping Forest landscape as you follow the broad rise through oak and hornbeam.

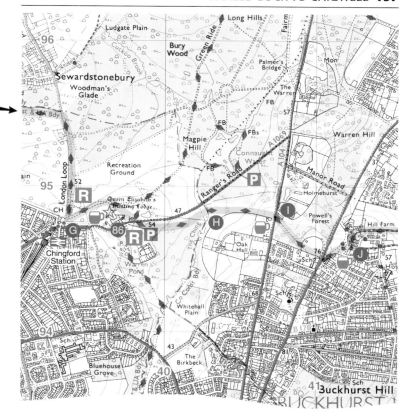

From Butler's Retreat, cross the road, the A1069, and turn immediately left on a track that runs near the road past a dignified stand of massive oaks. At a broad cross track, go a few paces right and continue over a log bridge to the foot of a wide, open grass slope **H**. Take one of the tracks that climb it to reach a road and the Warren Wood pub at the top. Cross the road and take the footpath that starts just right of a terrace of cottages **I**. The clear path climbs to the right of a clearing and through woodland to emerge beside a cricket field. Skirt along its edge to a road, the A121, where you cross and bear left, taking to the grass between two roads. Soon you are opposite the big Roebuck Hotel and you cross the grass to take the road just to its left. By the side of the Roebuck, just behind a pillar box, turn left through bollards onto an urban path **J**. It passes several cottages and comes to the bottom of a little lane, where your path continues ahead, well-concealed but running just right of a house garage.

Queen Elizabeth's Hunting Lodge was built primarily to provide a 'grandstand' view of hunting parties on Chingford Plain below.

The path curves right over a stile, then reveals itself as a fine old green track, dropping into the Roding Valley with a tree line to its left. The open fields to either side are further examples of 'buffer land' owned by the Corporation of London. Now you can hear the clatter of Central Line trains below you, and see the houses that they have brought spreading along the valley. Follow the left-hand edge of an open field, then take a footbridge over the railway at the bottom. Walk ahead to a road corner and turn left along Thaxted Road. Some way down, you can go right on a surfaced path **K** along a grassy strip between the houses to cross a road with the Mother Hubbard pub to your left, then over a second road and out into the Roding Valley open space. Keep ahead still to reach the banks of a lake. Attractive though it may look today, this lake was dug to provide the nearby M11 motorway workings with gravel!

Turn right along the lakeside path, bearing left with it around the head of the lake, to a footbridge over the Roding **87**. Quite a substantial river you will find here, but it is still surprising that, out in pastoral Essex where it gathers its waters, it gives its name to no fewer than eight 'Roding' villages. It finally flows, muddily, into the Thames at Barking Creek. Over the footbridge a rougher path continues with a steel sports-field fence to its right. It passes a car park, then joins the road leading from a big sports complex via an odd double kissing gate that seldom gets used. As you turn right with this road, you will notice the entrance to the Roding Valley Nature Reserve **88** on the corner – very tempting but, alas, only a diversion from the walk.

Coming up to a main road, turn left and cross over the M11. Keep on along the road, Chigwell Rise, crossing to the other footway if the opportunity arises for the views it offers across the Roding Valley. Nearing a crossing road, turn right into Brook Parade and on into the shops, with Chigwell station soon visible across the road. *At the crossing road, the LOOP route itself turns left towards old Chigwell village.*

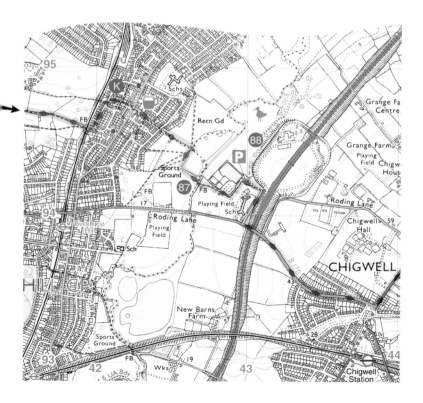

14 CHIGWELL TO HAROLD WOOD

10¾ miles (17.3 km) plus ¼ mile (0.4 km) of station link. You can leave the route at Havering-atte-Bower after 6 miles (9.6 km).

Chigwell is typical of a community that has grown up around its station, leaving the old village centre unspoilt and blissfully out of things. From the station **A**, turn right through the shops of Chigwell High Road, soon joining the main LOOP route as it comes along Chigwell Rise, across the mini-roundabout. Then it's up the hill, to discover a delightful little village group **89** at its top. As long as you keep the big Victorian addition hidden from view, St Mary is a typical church of rural Essex – its weatherboarded belfry topped by a broach spire. Alas, the Norman south door is hidden inside a modern, and firmly locked, porch. Facing it across the road is the Kings Head, a wondrous run of timber-framed inn, with elaborately carved bargeboards and little diamond-paned windows peeping out from an assortment of bays overhanging the pavement. The Kings Head is everyone's image of an ancient inn, and within one of those bays the Verderer's Court held its meetings, in the days when Chigwell lay deep in forest country.

A little way on, you are looking across to the long, mellow-brick schoolhouse of the grammar school, founded and endowed in 1629 by Samuel Harsnett, one-time vicar here, who, even when made Archbishop of York, thus remembered his home village. The master's house stands alongside the schoolroom, and Harsnett insisted that the occupant should be 'neither papist nor puritan . . . no tippler, haunter of alehouses or puffer of tobacco, but apt to teach and severe in punishment'. With a guilty suspicion that we would never have qualified, we take the footpath directly opposite the school, over a stile **B** and on with a bramble hedge to our right at first. This short path joins a road, which you cross rightwards to a gate leading to another footpath. Walk ahead, through a grove of trees and between two posts, out into open fields. Bear left now on a clear track, through a hedge gap to follow the field edge to your left, with a house in view in the trees ahead. Climbing, with views opening across the fertile Essex fields, often high with crop, the track comes to a meeting of ways just before the house, where you turn right, downhill.

Soon you turn left on a fine old green lane, Pudding Lane, wide enough between its hedges to have been a drove way. Where it gets less defined and begins to climb the rise ahead, turn right onto another track **C**, keeping a hedge to your left. Eventually the hedge ends, and then the track itself ends, and your path sets off half left over the brow of an open field, a line usually kept clear through the crop. Reaching the far side, the path joins another path just beyond the hedge line, to follow it rightwards beside the fence of a waterworks. This path emerges by the gates where a drive enters the waterworks. Cross the drive and take the grass path that continues beside their fence, with reservoir pools just to your left. The path runs beside a line of evergreens, coming to a stile on the right **D**. Cross it and walk with a hedge to your left, over two more stiles to pass a house, then along the right side of a lush, small meadow to another path that runs between a hedge and a fence, to the foot of a little lane. This is Chapel Lane, and the chapel itself, with a charming yellow-brick Victorian front, is beside you as you come up to the road at Chigwell Row.

If you had come to Chigwell Row in the early 19th century, you would have found a little community on the edge of another vast royal hunting forest. Unfortunately, Hainault Forest never found local defenders of the doughty character that saved its neighbour, Epping Forest, and after Parliament gave its consent in 1858, over 100,000 forest trees were felled and the land drained and fenced. The country park you walk through now is just a surviving fragment of Hainault Forest. Turn left along Lambourne Road and soon cross to take a concrete path out into the open space. Follow it as it curves right, down to the trees, then turns left to follow the woodland edge. When the concrete ends, keep on over grass, passing a children's play area. The Victorian church **90** up ahead was built on forest land, and the cream building to its left over the crossroads is the Maypole pub.

Just short of the road, turn right along the grass strip hedged off from it. Just before the grass ends, go through a kissing gate on the left and cross the road to another gate just to the right into Hainault Country Park. Take the middle of three rather faint paths **E** over open ground and into the trees. Through a gate, the path enters a fenced area, then keeps ahead down the left-hand side of an open field. At the bottom corner, cross a major track and, still keeping to the same direction, take to a horseride that drops gently through young, mainly

The distant tree-clad slopes are all that remain of Hainault Forest, seen here from the open grass of the country park.

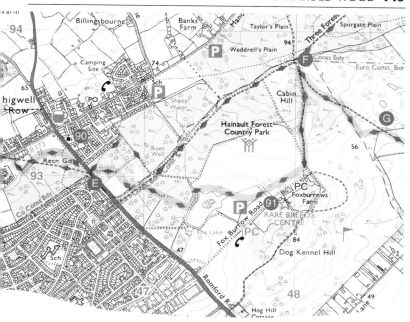

birch, woodland to the lake. Turn left along the track by the waterside, keeping on over grass by the lake, when the track turns away. Now a fine sweep of open grass comes down from the distant tree line to the lake, giving you a rare sense of freedom as you follow along its foot. *Passing a car park, the Country Park offices* **91** *and toilets are up to your right.* Nearing the end of this open stretch, bear left, aiming well left of a terrace of cottages, to find a surfaced track just inside the trees. Turn left on it to climb just inside the park boundary, with a golf-course fence to your right.

At the top, where the track levels out, go over a stile on the right **F** onto the golf course. Walk just left of a tiny grove of trees to enter a long tree belt, the Mile Plantation, already guided by waymarks and yellow bands on the trees. Within the tree belt turn right on a track, but almost immediately fork left on a less formal path which keeps safely within the trees until, over a prominent crossing track, it bears left and out into the open. Now the path goes through another tiny grove, drops down over a fairway with a green just to its right, and ahead you can see the corner of a fence and hedge that marks the edge of the golf course. Walk to the corner, then down the left-hand side to find a stile **G**, hidden away in foliage, leading out into the fields beyond.

A cottage with tiny 'post-box' replica at Havering-atte-Bower.

Over the stile, the path goes half left down a field, aiming for the corner of an old field boundary ditch. The view ahead now is to the tree-clad ridge of Havering Country Park, with the tower blocks of Romford over to the right, reminding you of the nearness of civilisation. Reaching the corner, continue with the ditch to your left, turning left when the field ends, still with the ditch to your left. This brings you to a metalled drive, and you turn right to follow it through a ramshackle farm area and past a much smarter house to a point where the ways divide. Turn left here, then when the drive goes right, keep ahead on the often-muddy bridleway. Coming to the country-park boundary, turn left up the rise, then, soon after passing a bench with panoramic views, go right through a wooden barrier **H** onto a path through the woods. Follow it straight on, and prepare for the awesome moment when you realise that giant redwoods **92** are towering above you. These majestic trees, the giant sequoia, or Wellingtonia, became fashionable after being 'discovered' during the Californian Gold Rush, and the avenue you now walk up once led to the mansion of Havering Park. The hundred sequoia around you here are relative youngsters and will grow much taller, but this is the second largest plantation in England.

At the '5 Ways' crossing keep ahead along the avenue, leaving the park for an unmade road. Before the buildings obscure it, look left for the amazing view over miles of Roding Valley countryside, then keep ahead between riding school and church, out to the little green of Havering-atte-Bower. It's worth crossing the green to the far corner, not only to admire the village stocks and whipping post preserved there, but to savour the equally stunning view south over Bedford Park and Romford. This is indeed a hilltop village, and in medieval times a royal palace sprawled over much of the high ground – a favoured spot for hunting in the forests around. The flint Victorian church **93** by the green is believed to occupy the site of one of the palace chapels, but otherwise not a stone, not a trace, remains. *There are toilets by the church, and just across the green a bus stop with services down to Romford station.*

From the green, bear left down the B175 road to pass the Royal Oak pub. Just beyond it, a footpath sign on the right points to a path **I** just before a cream bungalow. At first you wonder where the path is, but it squeezes just left of a brick garage and out into open fields.

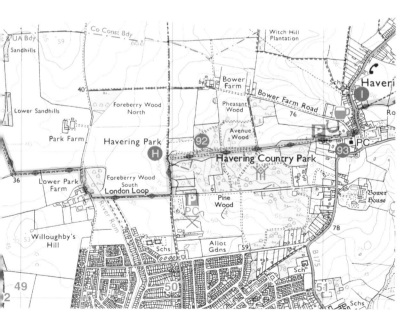

Keep to the right-hand field boundary now, through a kissing gate and up towards an odd, white roundhouse, a building that has been likened to a tea caddy. Keep following the boundary as it drops leftwards, then, at a kink in the hedge some way down, go right via a kissing gate **J** and a footbridge. Straight ahead now, over the rise of an open field to reach the left-hand end of a tree belt, then on via a track towards more woodland, passing a lone tree in midfield. Reaching the further trees, turn right to follow their edge, passing the overgrown remains of magnificent iron gateposts **94** that once graced an entrance to Pyrgo Park. Up a rise, you soon turn left to keep by the woodland edge, turning left again with the trees to reach a stile **K**. Here you are on a ridge, with park-like folds dropping away impressively to the south.

An unexpected touch of elegance: this iron gatepost in the fields above Havering-atte-Bower once graced an entrance to Pyrgo Park.

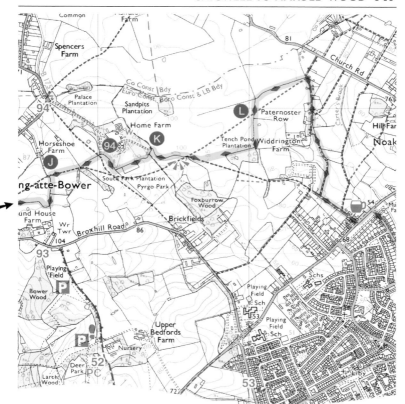

Turn right along the ridge track, keeping a fence to your left, going through a gate, then an old-style kissing gate, to turn right in the next field. Briefly you walk with the fence to your right, but then a grass track sets off leftward across the open field, aiming for the left-hand corner of a small wood. At the corner, keep straight on, the trees to your right. At the field end turn left, then some way on go right over a simple footbridge **L** and keep on, now with a hedge and ditch to your left. A stile takes you into a peaceful lane with the charming name of Paternoster Row, where you turn right. Pass several houses, then, just before the gates of Widdrington Farm, take the stile on the left onto a broad green track that runs confidently on until a stile beside a gate leads into another lane. A left turn brings you down to a main road, right beside the Bear pub. *From the bus stop opposite the pub, several services run frequently to Harold Wood and Romford stations.*

Turn left in Noak Hill Road, past the Bear, then right into Tees Drive. Just past the Priory Road turning, drop down leftwards to a path **M** beside Carter's Brook, here flowing in a steep-sided sylvan dell, quite unexpected in its urban setting. It will have several changes of name, but finally (as the Ingrebourne) you will be following this water down to the Thames. At the first crossing road, go over the brook and keep on beside it, now over grass. At the next crossing road, go through the gates into Central Park **95** and follow the metalled path as it first heads left, then bends back to rejoin the brook. Don't cross it here, but keep on with the brook to your right, passing a children's play area to exit into another crossing road. Keep on over grass again, with the brook still to your right, then over yet another road to pass a children's playground to your left. Now there is a big dual carriageway to cross, the A12 Colchester Road. The exit from the grass strip you are walking along is via a gate **N** up to your left, leading to a crossing point. If the traffic makes a crossing here seem hazardous, there is a pedestrian crossing some way up to your right.

Having reached the other side, an entry just to the left of the crossing point leads to one last open strip. Your path goes left of a grassy hump carrying children's slides, then becomes an enclosed track circuiting around the Paine's Brook Play Area (the brook has changed its name already!). Taking the drive out to a road, Church Road, turn right to cross the brook, then go left into Queens Park Road, following it as it turns right through a car barrier. Where Queens Park Road ends, keep ahead in Station Road, passing the King Harold pub and turning up left to Harold Wood station. *The LOOP continues past the station to turn left into Oak Road.*

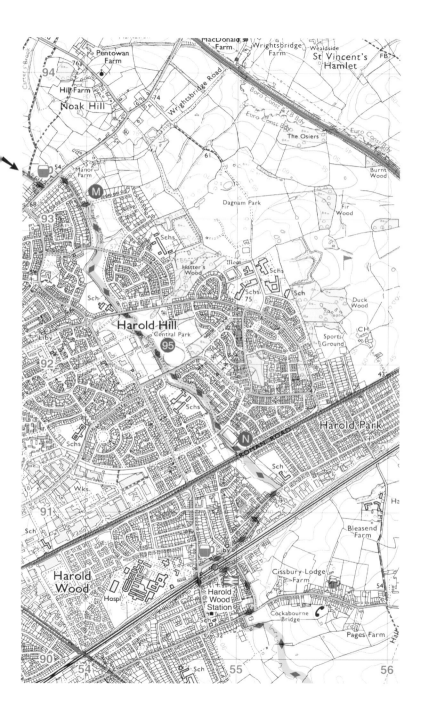

15 HAROLD WOOD TO COLDHARBOUR POINT

11¾ miles (19 km). You can leave the route at Upminster Bridge station after 4½ miles (7.2 km), or Rainham station after 9½ miles (15.3 km)

Having got this far around the LOOP, you have surely worked up a gritty determination to finish it. Which is just as well, as this section can involve long stretches of temporary road diversions. But, as always, the LOOP offers compensations, even some surprises, and nothing can detract from the final grandeur of the Thames estuary, so set off by turn-ing left from Harold Wood station exit **A**, and left again into Oak Road. *You are already on the LOOP route, which passes the station.*

Take Archibald Road, the third turning on the right, which turns out to be an unmade road, soon with open prospects over a gentle valley. The Paine's Brook has already added its waters to the Ingrebourne, which wanders through the rough grass, just to your left. Coming up to a busier road, turn right and very soon cross to go down a modest little turning, Brinsmead Road, opposite. It brings you to gates into Harold Wood Park **96**, where you turn left immediately on a surfaced track. When it ends, bear right along a grass strip and soon, on the left, you will come to a foot-bridge **B** over the Ingrebourne. Cross and turn right along the edge of the grass, and soon you will find a stile leading out of the park – the start of a permissive path by the river. Over the stile, circuit to the right around the field edge and begin following the meanders of the Ingrebourne. The little river, deep within its tunnel of lush foliage, may seldom show itself, but the occasional waymark post and a stile or two will guide you.

After a while, the path turns up briefly left by a field edge to come to a three-way fingerpost near an electricity pylon. Turn here and pass beneath the pylon into the next field, on the path signed 'To footpath 117'. It goes rightwards to rejoin the banks of the Ingrebourne briefly until, coming to a footbridge **C**, you do not cross but keep ahead up the field, having now joined the mysterious 'footpath 117'. It follows field edges up to Hall Lane, which you can enter either via a tempting hedge gap, or via the official stile along to the left. 'Footpath 117 to Southend Arterial Road' says the fingerpost here. No wonder they were so coy about telling you where footpath 117 was going!

However you enter Hall Lane, turn right and cross to the footway side. Coming to a road junction, take to the grass verge and bear left to follow Hall Lane as it crosses a major road, the A127. Over a slip road, the same verge takes you past The Strawberry Farm with its farm shop,

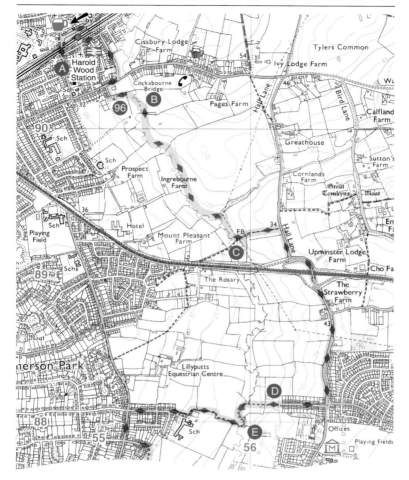

and on until you come to a mini-roundabout. Cross via the pedestrian island here, and almost immediately go right into River Drive. At the bottom, a stony path **D** squeezes between posts and drops through the woods, then over a meadow to a footbridge over the Ingrebourne. Over the bridge, turn left to follow the field edge near the river. As this big field ends, a useful-looking path leads ahead, but the right of way turns right **E** and up towards the buildings of Emerson Park School you can see above you. With a fence to your left, pass the school and reach the bottom of a road, Wych Elm Road. Keep ahead up the road, turning left at the crossroads, and then first left again into Rayburn Road. This soon ends, and you find a track continuing ahead, with almost immediately a footpath **F** setting off right, into the trees. It emerges on a crossing track and you go right, then left at a gate on a path along the top of the field, with views across the gentle Ingrebourne Valley. Where the field ends, the path drops briefly, then goes on between garden fences to the corner of a road. Keep ahead in the road, then, when it joins a main road, continue over a railway bridge. Immediately over the bridge, turn left into Minster Way, turning left again when it ends, into Upminster Road, *with shops and Upminster Bridge station just across the road.*

The LOOP continues down the main road, under the railway bridge and past the Bridge House pub just beyond. You cross the Ingrebourne, then turn right into Bridge Avenue. If, instead of turning, you keep on along the main road for a few minutes, across the road you will see Upminster Mill **97**, a fine example of a smock windmill that may soon be restored to working order. It is only open on occasional weekends in spring and summer. Some way up Bridge Avenue, you come to the gates of Hornchurch Sports Stadium on the right, where you turn down their drive and bear left into a car park area. On the left, beyond a car barrier, a metalled path **G** begins along the green strip beside the Ingrebourne known as Gaynes Parkway. At a triangular junction of ways, keep ahead, then cross the river via a footbridge and continue, now with the Ingrebourne to your left. Pedestrian lights take you across a busy road and straight on, bearing left back to the riverside, following the Ingrebourne Valley Green Way.

When the Green Way track goes through a gate and begins to turn up rightwards, you are entering Hornchurch Country Park **98**. Very soon you fork left, leaving a children's play area to your right, and take to the perimeter track on its bank above the river, following the direction sign to Albyns Farm. Now the Ingrebourne opens up into a series of lakes and reed swamps **99**, and several viewing bays invite you to linger and indulge in some bird-spotting. When floodwater fills this area in winter, it forms the largest freshwater marsh in London – an important nature reserve.

Topping a gentle rise, the track gives its broadest views of the Ingrebourne Marshes in their dip of valley – but in the foreground an incongruous element, a concrete pillbox, reminds you that you are on the edge of a Battle of Britain airfield. Indeed the first flying here was in World War I, when Suttons Farm was taken over by the Royal Flying Corps to defend London from the Zeppelin raids. The Royal Air Force took over a larger area, and the Hornchurch Spitfires played a major role, especially when bomber fleets thundered up the Thames estuary in 1940. Today's country park was opened in 1980, relandscaping the scene after it had been quarried and used as a huge landfill site.

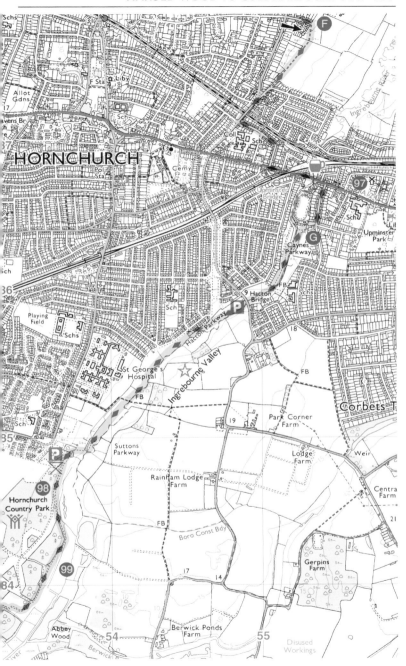

Don't take any of the tracks branching right, but keep along the bank top until your track finally turns up right **H** and reaches the lakeside, with Albyns Farm **100** in view across the water. Follow the track still, keeping the lake to your right, then bear right with it, up to the farm. *In a few years the LOOP will be able to continue by the Ingrebourne, but this will not be possible until another landfill site has been restored and opened.* For the present, go past a gate and take to the farm drive. Where the drive turns right, keep ahead on a footpath **I** leading to Avelon Road. Turn left here to walk with flats to your right and open land to your left until, just before Avelon Road clearly ends, you turn right. Now you are in Grove Park Road, leading up to a busier highway, South End Road. Turn left now, *and pass a bus stop from which, if you want to avoid a road walk, the service 165 will take you on to Rainham.*

Gluttons for punishment will carry on to a major traffic-light junction, turning left into Rainham Road. Keeping on to an even bigger roundabout where your road meets the A13, bear right with the pavement to go under the main road via a pedestrian subway. On the other side, go left up the slope and bear right, soon crossing the Ingrebourne one last time, and coming into Rainham village. Two pubs, the Bell and the New Angel, face one another, with a third, the Phoenix, a little further on.

Looking from the river wall at Rainham Ferry, the mudflats and open skies of the Thames estuary make a vast panorama.

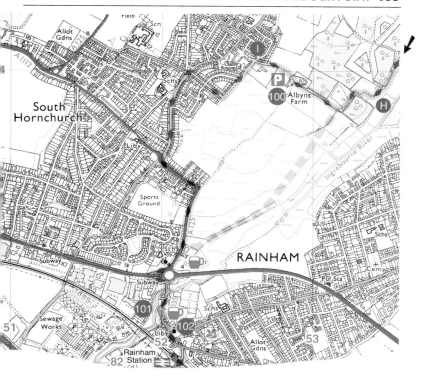

Opposite the Bell, it is well worth turning briefly into the new park where you can meet the waters of Rainham Creek **101** and gain some sense of the relationship little Rainham once had with the distant Thames. Right up to the 19th century, the creek was navigable for sailing barges, and a wealthy sea captain, John Harle, not only owned the wharves here, but used the profits to have the handsome Rainham Hall built in 1729, at the heart of the village. It stands proudly behind its iron gates, next to the churchyard of St Helen and St Giles **102**, a rare example of a complete late-Norman church. The broad, stumpy tower has little slits of Norman windows, a tiny Norman doorway can still be seen in the chancel wall, and much of the rubble stonework is literally black with age.

One day the path by Rainham Creek will take us to the Thames, but currently it goes nowhere, so keep on through the village, passing Rainham Hall and forking right into Ferry Lane to reach the station. *The LOOP now continues to the Thames and Coldharbour Point, but then has to return to this station, so you have a good excuse for breaking off here!*

The tower blocks of Erith across the estuary stand silhouetted against the evening sun, while a concrete barge lies stranded on nearby mud.

To complete the LOOP journey, walk over the level crossing and on along Ferry Lane, crossing to the footway side. There are strange contrasts now. To your left, the straggly expanse of Rainham Marsh **103**, with the occasional gleam of water from a drainage ditch in amongst the tall grasses. To your right, the all-too-familiar estuary clutter of scrap-metal dealers, car breakers and salvage yards, culminating in a range of low heather-clad hills that turn out, on closer inspection, to be mountains of rusty containers. How they stack them so high, and what would happen if you removed one from the bottom? These are questions to ponder, as you pass beneath them.

Go under a bypass on stilts, crossing a couple of slip roads in the process, and continue along Ferry Lane South. When eventually a grass bank appears on the right, cross and climb the steps to a signed riverside path **J**. Rather belying its title, it passes a lorry park, then a yard full of sad, unwanted buses until, climbing to a concrete flood wall, the broad estuary is at last revealed. A just reward for our efforts, and happily the scale of the scene transcends all this junk we pile beside it. Follow the river bank now, with the silos of the Tilda Rice plant up ahead. Steps **K** take you over a flood wall and past their working frontage. Then in a shallow bay comes an eerie sight – a big family of barges, abandoned on the mud **104**. But no ordinary barges. These are made of concrete, first towed across the channel as part of the Mulberry Harbour that supported the D-Day landings of World War II. In 1953 they served a second duty, shoring up the estuary flood defences, but now nobody wants them any more.

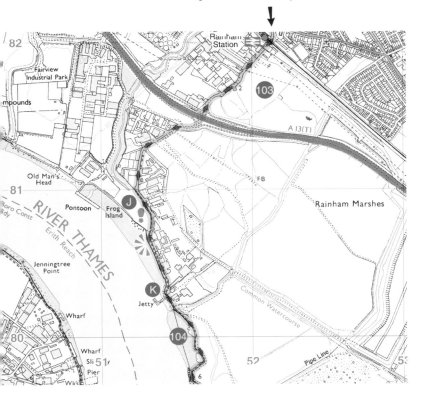

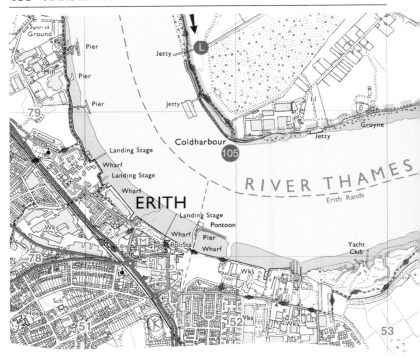

The LOOP stops here. Beyond the barrier, a lonely beacon tower marks Coldharbour Point, with the Thames now widening to greet the sea.

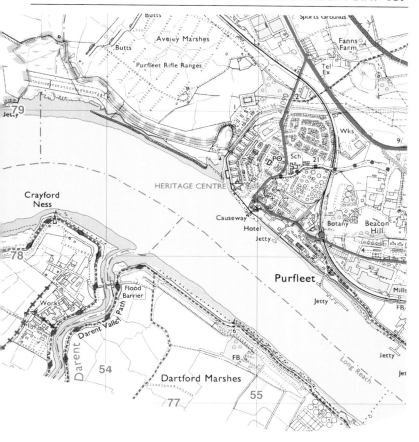

The path takes a gated footbridge over a sludge pipeline **L**, then crosses the road access to a big waste-transfer wharf, keeping ahead over grass towards the distant beacon tower on Coldharbour Point **105**. Here you are walking beneath gentle slopes of grass, and you would hardly guess that these are newly grassed-over rubbish tips – London's rubbish that came in container barges to the wharf. *One day, the riverside path will continue beyond the point to Purfleet, but until the signs confirm that a new path is open, our LOOP journey ends here and we must retrace our steps to Rainham station.* Across the Thames you can easily spot the pier and Erith river front where the journey began. On the river wall at the foot of Ferry Lane is a plaque to commemorate the founding of the ancient Rainham-to-Erith Ferry in 1199 AD. If it still ran, the LOOP would be using it!

USEFUL
INFORMATION

TRANSPORT

Taking a walk on the LOOP is an occasion for leaving the car at home and making use of London's good public transport links. For many walkers, the most economical way of doing this will be to set out with the appropriate Travelcard. The list of public transport access points below tells you the Zone each one falls in.

Travelcards

The one-day Travelcard is valid after 9.30 am Monday to Friday, and any time at weekends or on public holidays. For adults the cost varies according to the number of zones you want to travel through, but there is a flat rate for children aged five to 15. There are several other kinds of Travelcard, for example a Weekend Travelcard will save you 25 per cent on the cost of two ordinary cards, and can be used for the two days of an ordinary weekend, or on two consecutive days of a public-holiday weekend. A Family Travelcard offers a saving on individual Travelcards when one or two adults are travelling with up to four children, with a very low flat rate for the children. They needn't be related, but must travel together.

You can buy Travelcards at tube stations, most London rail stations, London Transport Information Centres, and at over 2,300 pass agents around London, usually local newsagents displaying the 'Pass Agent' sign. There are six zones in total, and when you buy your card you need to state which zones you aim to travel through. The more zones, the more the card costs, with Zone 1, Central London, being relatively more expensive. The bus network is divided into four zones. Bus Zone 4 is an outer zone covering approximately the same area for bus travel as Zones 4, 5 and 6 combined on the Underground and national rail network.

Travel Information

Our list of public transport access points gives an indication of the likely frequency of service, but this can only serve as a general guide – timetables change, bus route numbers and frequencies can also change. Where services are infrequent, we strongly advise checking first. For detailed information on London Transport tube and bus services, ring 020 7222 1234. For national rail information, train times, etc, ring 08457 484950. Both these are 24-hour services.

The staging points

These are the major staging points along the London LOOP, with the Travelcard Zones they fall in, major destinations the services run to, and the frequency of service you can expect through the middle of the day, in terms of number of trains/buses/trams per hour. W = Weekdays, S = Saturday, Sun = Sundays.

Zone

6   **Erith stn.** Connex to London Bdge, Waterloo E., Charing X. 4 W and S, 2 Sun.

6   **Crayford stn.** Connex to London Bdge, Waterloo E., Charing X, Cannon St. 4 W and S, 2 Sun.

6   **Bexley stn.** Connex to London Bdge, Waterloo E., Charing X, Cannon St. 4 W and S, 2 Sun.

4   **Foots Cray.** Buses to Eltham and Sidcup stations.

4   **Queen Mary's Hospital.** Buses to Sidcup station.

5   **Petts Wood stn.** Connex to London Bdge, Waterloo E., Charing X, Victoria. 7 W, 6 S, 4 Sun.

4   **Farnborough.** Buses 261 and 358 to Bromley or Orpington.

5   **Hayes stn.** Connex to London Bdge, Waterloo E., Charing X. 2 W and S, 1 Sun.

4   **Upper Shirley.** Bus 130 to E. Croydon stn. 8 W and S, 5 Sun.

6   **Coombe Lane stn.** Tramlink to E. Croydon stn. 8 W and S, 4 Sun.

4   **Selsdon Park Road.** Bus 64 to E. Croydon stn. 6 W and S, 3 Sun.

4   **Hamsey Green.** Bus 403 to central Croydon. 5 W and S, 3 Sun.

4   **Coulsdon Common.** Buses 404, 409, 466 to Coulsdon S. and E. Croydon stns.

6   **Coulsdon South stn.** Connex to Clapham Jcn, Victoria. 2 W and S, 1 Sun.

*   **Banstead stn.** Connex to Clapham Jcn, Victoria. 1 W and S, No service Sun. **

*   **Ewell West stn.** South West Trains to Clapham Jcn, Waterloo. 2 W, S and Sun.

4   **Malden Manor stn.** South West Trains to Clapham Jcn, Waterloo. 2 W, S and Sun.

* Outside Travelcard Zones
** On Sundays, best to divert to Belmont station (Zone 6, or 4 for buses) where bus 280 runs to Sutton station, 5 W and S, 4 Sun.

5   **Berrylands stn.** South West Trains to Clapham Jcn, Waterloo. 2 W, S and Sun.

6   **Kingston stn.** South West Trains to Clapham Jcn, Waterloo. 6 W and S, 3 Sun.

6   **Fulwell stn.** South West Trains to Clapham Jcn, Waterloo. 2 W and S, 1 Sun.

4   **Hanworth Road.** Bus 111 to Heathrow, Hounslow, Kingston. 5 W and S, 4 Sun.

5   **Hatton Cross stn.** Piccadilly Line (Heathrow). 7 to 14 W and S, 7 Sun.

5   **Hayes & Harlington stn.** Thames Trains to Ealing Bdway, Paddington. 4 W and S, 2 Sun.

6   **West Drayton stn.** Thames Trains to Ealing Broadway, Paddington. 2 W, S and Sun.

6   **Uxbridge stn**. Metropolitan Line. 6 W and S, 4 Sun. Also Piccadilly Line, peak hours.

4   **Harefield West.** Bus U9 to Uxbridge. 2 W and S. Bus 331 from Harefield village, 2 Sun.

6   **Moor Park stn.** Metropolitan Line. 9 W and S, 7 Sun.

6   **Hatch End stn.** Silverlink to Euston. 3 W and S, 2 Sun.

5   **Stanmore stn.** Jubilee Line. 7 to 10 W and S, 4 Sun.

6   **Elstree & Borehamwood stn.** Thameslink to King's X. 4 W and S, 2 Sun.

5   **High Barnet stn.** Northern Line. 5 W, S and Sun.

5   **Cockfosters stn.** Piccadilly Line. 12 to 15 W, S and Sun.

5   **Gordon Hill stn.** WAGN to Finsbury Pk, Moorgate. 3 W, 2 S, 1 Sun (to King's X).

6   **Turkey Street stn.** WAGN to Liverpool St. 2 W and S. No service Sun.

6   **Enfield Lock stn.** WAGN to Liverpool St. 2 W and S, 1 Sun.

5   **Chingford stn.** WAGN to Liverpool St. 4 W, 3 S, 2 Sun.

5   **Chigwell stn.** Central Line via Woodford. 3 W, 2 S and Sun. No evening service.

4   **Havering-atte-Bower.** Buses 500/502 to Romford stn. 2 W and S, 1 Sun.

6   **Harold Wood stn.** First Great Eastern to Liverpool St. 6 W and S, 3 Sun.

6   **Upminster Bridge stn.** District Line. 6 W, S and Sun.

6   **Rainham stn.** C2C to Fenchurch St. 2 W and S, 1 Sun.

USEFUL ADDRESSES

British Waterways, Willow Grange, Church Road, Watford WD1 3QA. Tel: 01923 226422. Fax: 01923 201400. E-mail: enquiries.hq@britishwaterways.co.uk Net: www.britishwaterways.co.uk *Administers the canal system, including the Grand Union Canal.*

Corporation of London, Guildhall, Barbican EC2P 2EJ. Tel: 020 7606 3030. *Owns and manages many open spaces in and near London.*

Epping Forest Information Centre, High Beach, Loughton IG10 4AF. Tel: 020 8508 0028. Fax: 020 8532 0188. *For guided walks and publications.*

West Wickham and Coulsdon Commons, Merlewood Estate Office, Ninehams Road, Caterham-on-the-Hill CR3 5LN. Tel: 020 8660 8533. Fax: 020 8763 8598.

Countryside Agency, John Dower House, Crescent Place, Cheltenham GL50 3RA Tel: 01242 521381. Fax: 01242 584270. E-mail: enquiries@countryside.govt.uk   Net: www.countryside.gov.uk

South East & London Region, Dacre House, 19 Dacre Street, London SW1H 0DH. Tel: 020 7340 2900. Fax: 020 7340 2999.

London Walking Forum, 3rd Floor, 31–33 Bondway, Vauxhall, London SW8 1SJ. Tel: 020 7582 4071. Fax: 020 7820 8208. E-mail: info@londonwalking.com   Net: www.londonwalking.com *Information on all London walks.*

London Wildlife Trust, Harling House, 47–51 Great Suffolk Street, London SE1 0BS. Tel: 020 7261 0447. Fax: 020 7261 0538. E-mail: londonwt@cix.co.uk *Care for over 50 nature reserves in Greater London including several along the LOOP.*

London Green Belt Council, 13 Oakleigh Park Avenue, Chislehurst BR7 5PB. Tel: 020 8467 5346.

Long Distance Walkers Association, Tom Sinclair, Bank House, High Street, Wrotham TN15 7AE. Tel: 01732 883705. E-mail: tom@bankhouse.f9.co.uk

National Trust, PO Box 39, Bromley BR1 3XL. Tel: 020 8315 1111. Fax: 020 8466 6824. E-mail: enquiries@ntrust.org.uk *For membership and general enquiries.*

Blewcoat School, 23 Caxton Street, Westminster SW1H 0PY. Tel: 020 7222 2877. *For information about Trust properties in Greater London.*

Open Spaces Society, 25A Bell Street, Henley-on-Thames RG9 2BA.
Tel: 01491 573535. E-mail: osshq@aol.com
Net: www.oss.org.uk *Protects common land, greens and open spaces.*

Ordnance Survey, Romsey Road, Southampton SO16 4GU.
Tel: 08456 050505. Fax: 023 8079 2615.
E-mail: enquiries@ordsvy.gov.uk   Net: www.ordsvy.gov.uk

Ramblers' Association, 2nd Floor, Camelford House, 87–90 Albert
Embankment, London SE1 7TW. Tel: 020 7339 8500. Fax: 020 7339 8501.
E-mail: ramblers@london.ramblers.org.uk   Net: www.ramblers.org.uk
Takes up path problems and organises walks via a network of local groups.

Youth Hostels Association, Trevelyan House, 8 St Stephen's Hill,
St Albans AL1 2DY. Tel: 01727 855215. Net: www.yha.org.uk *Have
several hostels offering low-cost accommodation in Central London.*

Tourist Information Centres can help with local accommodation,
transport and details of places to visit, etc:

Bexley, The Visitor Centre, Hall Place, Bourne Road, Bexley DA5 1PQ.
Tel: 01322 526574. Fax: 01322 52292.

Bromley, Central Library, High Street, Bromley BR1 1EX.
Tel: 020 8460 9955. Fax: 020 8313 9975.

Croydon, Croydon Clocktower, Katherine Street, Croydon CR9 1ET.
Tel: 020 8253 1009. Fax: 020 8253 1008. E-mail: tic@library.croydon.gov.uk

Harrow, Civic Centre, Station Road, Harrow HA1 2XF. Tel: 020 8424
1102. Fax: 020 8424 1134. E-mail: info@harrow.gov.uk

Hillingdon, Central Library, 14–15 High Street, Uxbridge UB8 1HD.
Tel: 01895 250706. Fax: 01895 239794.

Hounslow, The Treaty Centre, High Street, Hounslow TW3 1ES.
Tel: 020 8572 8279. Fax: 020 8569 4330.

Kingston, The Market House, Market Place, Kingston upon Thames
KT1 1JS. Tel: 020 8547 5592. Fax: 020 8547 5594.

Richmond, Old Town Hall, Whittaker Avenue, Richmond TW9 1TP.
Tel: 020 8940 9125. Fax: 020 8940 6899. Email: info@richmond.gov.uk

Colne Valley Park Visitor Centre, Denham Court Drive, Denham,
Uxbridge, UB9 5PG. Tel: 01895 833375. Fax: 01895 833552.
For walks and other countryside events along the Colne Valley.

Lea Valley Park Information Centre, Abbey Gardens, Waltham
Abbey EN9 1XQ. Tel: 01992 702200. Fax: 01992 702330.

BIBLIOGRAPHY

The London Encyclopaedia, Weinreb, Ben and Hibbert, Christopher. Macmillan, revised edition 1993. *The standard reference work covering Greater London.*

The Buildings of England, London 2: South, 3: North West, 4: North, 5: East and Docklands, Cherry, Bridget and Pevsner, Nikolaus. Penguin. *The authoritative record of all significant buildings in Greater London.*

Village London, Past and Present, Grant, Neil, in association with the Francis Frith Collection, extra photography by Nick Wright. Octopus, 1990. *Brief histories of London suburbs and environs, with 'old and new' illustrations.*

Two reprints of Victorian guides give fascinating insights into the development of Outer London communities:

Handbook to the Environs of London, Thorne, James. Originally published 1876. Reprinted 1983 by Godfrey Cave.

Village London, Walford, Edward. Originally published 1883–4 under the title *Greater London*. Reprinted in four parts by The Alderman Press, 1985.

Two classic books give an overview of London's wildlife and how it has adapted to change:

London's Natural History, Fitter, Richard S. R. Published in the Collins New Naturalist series 1945, reprinted by Bloomsbury, 1990.

The Naturalist in London, Burton, John A. David & Charles, 1974.

ORDNANCE SURVEY MAPS COVERING THE LONDON LOOP

Landranger Maps (scale: 1:50 000): 176, 177, 187.
Explorer Maps (scale: 1:25 000): 162 Greenwich & Gravesend, 147 Sevenoaks & Tonbridge, 161 London South, 146 Dorking, Box Hill & Reigate, 160 Windsor, Weybridge & Bracknell, 172 Chiltern Hills East, 173 London North, 174 Epping Forest & Lea Valley, 175 Southend-on-Sea & Basildon.